IMMERSED IN WEST AFRICA

My Solo Journey Across Senegal, Mauritania, The Gambia, Guinea and Guinea Bissau

TERRY LISTER

Book Power Publishing is a division of Niyah Press
www.bookpowerpublishing.com

Bulk purchases are available for schools and groups.
For information, please email the author at TerryLister01@gmail.com

ISBN: 978-1-945873-19-5

The very basic core of a man's living spirit is his passion for adventure. The joy of life comes from our encounters with new experiences, and hence there is no greater joy than to have an endlessly changing horizon, for each day to have a new and different sun.

From **Into the Wild** *by Jon Krakauer.*

THIS BOOK IS dedicated to the memory of the man who taught me by word and deed. As I travel, so many times his words of guidance come to mind and direct my footsteps all these years later. I was very blessed to have Eugene Lister as my father. He was a man of integrity who did not have to shout to get his points across, instead he had a calmness that made you pay attention. Long before GPS, he would say, "Terry as long as you have gas in the tank, enough sunlight and you have established landmarks, you will never get lost." Good advice which I follow to this day even though GPS exists!

CONTENTS

INTRODUCTION

I COME FROM A family of travellers. Dad and Mom travelled far and wide and, most importantly, frequently. My dad's brothers, my uncles Allan and Walter, were often "away," as there were always places to go and people to see. This was in my blood and I happily passed it onto my children who have been to many exotic places that I still hope to get to.

I'm from Bermuda, a very small island. We have an expression that basically says "He got rock fever," which means the person in question simply had to get off the island. So, as a people, we are well travelled. I can remember being home for the summer and running into one of my school friends who had gone to work after high school. He was 20 at the time. I asked how he was doing and what he was up to. He replied, "Not much. Working and a little bit of travel." I asked about his most recent trip and he said Hong Kong —a place I still have not been to!

When I was in primary school, we had a geography reader that was intended to expose us to the different parts of the world. Two characters from the book have stayed with me all my life. One was a little girl from South America with her llama and the other was Bombo, a little boy from Africa. Bombo has stayed in my subconscious, inspiring me to go see and learn for myself. As an eight-year-old, I was fascinated by the thought that I had descended from Africa, a place that I knew very little about.

I was a boy who loved sports and being outdoors but I was equally comfortable curled up with a book. Let me read about some foreign land and just imagine what that place was like. Oh, I wanted to go there! I remember being in the Galapagos Islands in 2016 and almost pinching myself. I read a lot about this place from boyhood but I never thought I would be there and there I was. I have had this travel bug all my life!

In my last year of high school, one of our school subjects was geography. Although I was good with the subject, it was a bit ironic, as I live in a tiny island that limited my exposure to the world beyond its confines. That summer following graduation, I went overseas to study. While flying over the Eastern Seaboard on my way to Toronto, I looked through the window of the airplane and saw lakes and winding rivers. I was excited because I had studied this and wrote about it but had never seen it in person. So the fire was stoked even more.

After my career and upon my retirement, I decided to go into a new direction. But first, to ensure that I would truly be retired, I surrendered both my licence to practice as an accountant and as a realtor. No longer can I act professionally in these areas. With that behind me, I set out to do what I had been planning for years. I took on a new vocation: that of a traveller.

To get the feel of it, to see if I would really like it or if I would find I had a silly dream which when put to the test fell apart, I started my journey in Central America. Close by, with its civil wars now history, I found beautiful people living in peace.

I had to decide what would be the right length of my trips to ensure I would get maximum enjoyment and experience. I tried six weeks, eight weeks and twelve weeks during my time in Central America and then South America. By trial and error, I found six weeks were too short, twelve weeks were too long, but eight weeks were just right.

Having found that I really enjoyed doing this vocation and having settled on the time spans, it was time to move on. After almost three years spent between my home, Bermuda, and Central and South America, I decided my next continent would be Africa. I had so many good reasons to choose Africa but the most important for me was to feel and experience the culture and history of the different countries.

Next I had to decide where to start. Would I follow the normal tourist routes or would I strike out on my own? If I wanted to follow the normal routes I could go to Mediterranean Africa and spend my time in Morrocco, Tunisa and Egypt. Or I could go to Southern Africa and enjoy Bots, South Africa and Namibia. Safaris and culture to enjoy here. Or I could go to East Africa and allow the adventures available in Kenya, Tanzania and Uganda to fill my soul. But after thinking about this I decided to go off trail and head for West Africa. Of course, Senegal and Ghana present wonderful tourism opportunities but the bulk of the other countries remain undiscovered.

So West Africa. But where in West Africa? I decided that I would experience the history and culture of Senegal first and then work my way through Mauritania, The Gambia and the two Guineas. I wanted to see how these people, largely untouched by tourism, lived their lives and celebrated both their triumphs and their failures. Today, after two years of continual travel in Africa, I know I started in the right area.

Travel is such an eye-opener. It is almost impossible to visit some other place and return without having learned something. When we do not travel we remain set in our ways believing that the way we do it is the only way to do it. Over the years, just by travelling and observing, I have seen so many things that I knew would be of benefit to my own country.

The world we live in is so interconnected that individuals should take the opportunity to see the place from which the interconnections that matter in their lives are coming from. This will lead to greater understanding. This certainly applies to the people side. As we sit in our homes watching television, we form opinions that are directed by someone else. But when we get on the plane and go, we can form opinions based on criteria that matter to us.

Many people through sheer national pride think they live in the most beautiful place in the world. If put to the test, they can talk about all the wonderful things to see and do in their country. While this is all good, I would like to see people travelling so they can see the many beautiful sights that exist overseas. Some people need to see Niagara Falls, the Tower of London or the Eiffel Tower. But there are many other wonders that we could not see by sitting at home. I remember some years ago going to Jordan and, as much of a traveller as I am, prior to deciding to go I had never heard of Petra. Wow! What a place! And I had never heard of it. There are so many places that travel can expose us to and make us better people as a result.

Back in the 1980s and 1990s, experiencing black countries meant going to the Caribbean. By 1992, I realised that the Caribbean was changing and evolving into one that, in many ways, was like the USA mainland. With this in mind, that summer my children spent two weeks with their parents going to five islands to see the West Indies that had existed for much of the 19th and 20th centuries. I have carried this same concern regarding the African continent. I wanted to see and experience it before it changed into something else.

Africa has been called the Dark Continent since the 17th century or possibly before. The phrase has conjured up different images, depending on who said it and in what context. Many of the early European explorers used the term with a sense of wonder and mystery as they ventured out daily and saw new and marvellous things. Later, the exploiters had to paint a picture of the dark and heathen-infested place crawling with cannibals and spirit worshippers to justify the need to christen the native people. And justify they did.

These reasons, and more, have compelled me to go visit the continent.

I do not think anyone would disagree with the perception that Africa is a dangerous place. It has wars, health issues, and other dangers real or perceived. I believed the time to go was before I got too old to handle the challenge that Africa presents. In October 2017, I set out for West Africa to touch, taste, and smell for myself.

In writing this book, I want to expose my readers to what I found at the ground level. During this trip, I travelled as the locals travel, from riding in minivans that could comfortably take seven passengers, but instead were crammed with as many as fourteen people, to riding on the back of a moto with other passengers. By travelling as a solo or independent traveller, I have found it easy to become immersed in the local culture. This experience has been an eye-opener like no other. Among the benefits is gaining an insight into the daily challenges facing the average African.

My hope is that you will see, as I have seen, that while there are parts of Africa that continue to be dangerous, there are many that simply are not. Furthermore, you will see the beauty of these places and you will get a taste of their history and culture.

CHAPTER 1
SENEGAL

WITH 15 MILLION people, Senegal is on the rise. There is a flavour about it that fills not only your nose but your very soul. Be open to it. The history... Goree Island.... the culture.... the people... I experienced all of this during the first week of my trip while in Dakar, the exceptionally vibrant capital city. Witness the enthusiasm of the young boys who operate the mule carts and their slightly older brothers who operate the horses that race goods around various parts of the city.

This country, formerly a colony of France, has a richness that can only be understood by travelling there. From a refreshing swim in the Pink Lake to the villages be prepared for surprises. For one, the vast majority of people do not speak French. Instead, they speak the tribal language of Wolof. Thus, brushing up on your high school French will not help you get a cab most times!

As well as the horrors of history portrayed in Goree Island, the largest statue in Africa is located there in Dakar, the African Renaissance Monument. It stands as a tribute to the resiliency of the human spirit.

Read on and experience Senegal with me!

Les Mamelles Lighthouse

The Les Mamelles Lighthouse, on the outskirts of Dakar, Senegal's capital, was always an interesting place to visit. It is built on what is called the Deux Mamelles, the twin hills located in the suburban area of Ouakam, in Dakar. It is an interesting feature as the hills accentuate what's an otherwise flat landscape. On one hill, you'll find the Monument l'Renaissance Afrique (or African Renaissance Monument). On the other, the Mamelles Lighthouse.

I was keen to go up to the lighthouse after visiting the Monument. However, the day was already hot and I was hungry so I got some lunch. Having read that the walk up to the lighthouse took 20 minutes, I decided to flag a cab to take me. I was surprised that the driver, despite the strong likelihood that he had been driving past this unforgettable sight every day, did not know the way up and depended on me for directions!

The lighthouse is located in the western-most part of Africa. It was made operational in 1864 and to put it in the context of the times, it may well have provided crucial guidance for the ships that served the slave trade. Its light beam can be seen for 53 km and it has been described as one of the world's greatest lighthouses.

The lighthouse is 52 feet tall, and taking the hill's height in consideration, it has an elevation of 390 feet. There are two floors for operations and many cell towers, which are earning from the rental. Even today, the lighthouse is manned, not automated. There are four keepers who live in four cottages nearby with their wives and children.

This is an absolutely beautiful site for sightseeing. In fact, at night there is a band and a small restaurant and, although I did not get there myself, I was told that it is quite a nice spot for a night out. Having done my personal tour, and not having any other visitors come along, when I was ready to leave, I had to walk all the way down—it was so much easier than walking up. It was a pleasure to visit this lighthouse considering its place in history and its importance to Africa even today.

The African Renaissance Monument is the tallest statue in Africa and one of the largest in the world—it is even taller than the Statue of Liberty in New York or Rio's Christ the Redeemer.

Symbolizing 50 years of independence from France, the African Renaissance Monument stands some 169 feet. As previously mentioned, it is built on one of the two hills in the area known as the Deux Mamelles. Conceived by Senegal's President Abdoulaye Wade who received much criticism for it as the country's economy was in the doldrums at the time, the monument took four years (from 2006 to 2010) to be completed.

It is a bronze statue designed by the Senegalese but built by North Koreans who at the time of my trip had built nineteen such statues in African and Asian countries.

The African Renaissance Monument

When viewing, you have three options: first, view from the outside; second, going in and having a guided tour of the Monument even up to the third floor; and third, once you're on the third floor, you can enjoy the views through the windows. I chose to do the first two, but passed on the third.

Gorée Island

One Sunday, I made an emotional journey to Gorée, that infamous island with deep roots in the history of the slave trade. It is a small, car-free island off the coast of Dakar, still in Senegal. I did not know how I would react to the visit but I felt this was something that I must do.

Well, I wrote about the visit and attempted to post it on social media. For two subsequent days my phone said it was "still posting." Finally, when I looked at the phone I saw it had gone through. Great, I thought. But then I cannot find it! Terry = 0; Technology = 1. So I had to do it all over again.

Much like the trip I had taken many years ago to the infamous

Robben Island of South Africa, the oval island where Nelson Mandela spent years in isolation as a prisoner, I had to take a boat to reach Gorée. There was a very nice ferry that was filled with families and young couples going across to visit the island. It is a short 20-minute ride and before you even know it, you are already docking.

This now very famous island is merely 300 metres by 900 metres. It is indeed very small. About 1,200 people live there today selling their wares to visitors. Because of its location as the westernmost point of Africa, the island played a significant role in defending the continent during the colonial period. No wonder it has both a fort and a castle with three sets of guns.

During the terrible period of the slave trade, the island had 28 slave houses. Many still exist but these are now repurposed. The island was governed by the French who had no significant colonies in the New World but a very strong presence in West Africa. Consider the number of African nations that still currently use French as their official language.

The Maison des Esclaves, which can be found here and is a museum and memorial to the Atlantic slave trade that used to take place on Gorée, was renovated in 1990 and then opened for tours. More than two million Africans passed through Gorée Island to the New World. They came from all over West Africa. The practice of breaking up families that was heavily practiced in the New World was in full force here as family members ended up on different ships headed for different countries! Many died on Gorée refusing to submit, choosing death over transhipment.

The Maison des Esclaves has two floors. The upper would have been used by those responsible for holding the Africans before shipment. The lower floor is where the Africans were kept. Men, women, and children were all separate from one another. The men were held in very small rooms for 23 hours a day. They could be held there for as long as four months waiting for the next ship.

I saw the utterly cramped areas where they were kept for punishment. I was told that when Nelson Mandela visited Gorée, he asked to be allowed to enter one of these two spots. He stayed for ten minutes and came out in tears.

Later, I found myself face-to-face with the Door of No Return. Friends who have been to Gorée ahead of me told me how they wept as they stood there. I simply felt numb.

All that I have read over the years, all that I have experienced resulted in numbness. I invite you to make your own journey to experience for yourself.

Gorée Island's Amazing Artisans

When I thought of Gorée Island, I always focused on seeing the Door of No Return. I did not think of the island in any other way. So when my guide walked me around the rest of the island, I was taken aback a little by seeing the vendors with their craft!

During the tour, we came upon a man who did sand painting. He was kind enough to show us how he did it. The West African region had sands of 16 different hues or colours, which are perfect for this work. To start, the artisan decides what he wishes to make and then selects a board to serve as the base. The board is then painted with a glue from a young Baobab tree. Then the design is done by the artist sprinkling the different colours of sand in the desired shape unto the board. Once done, the artist knocks the design against his desk to remove the excess sand. The design needs only a few minutes to dry. I was quite impressed by the display of skill!

Last Thursday, I hired a driver who took me to Lake Retba, Senegal's so-called Pink Lake which is an hour's drive north of Dakar. The lake is famous for its colour in the dry season when it changes to be completely pink, one of only two such lakes in the world. What causes this is the high salinity of water being second only to that of the Dead Sea.

This is a popular tourist spot but the government has restricted the construction of new buildings, thus there are only two hotels here. I was taken to one of the hotels where an hour-long tour on a neat 4X4 vehicle was arranged. The season was such that the lake was only partially pink but this will change in the coming weeks.

The biggest economic activity at Lake Retba is the harvesting of the salt. I have previously seen this done outside of Cusco in Peru and on the salt flats of Bolivia. Each country takes its own unique approach to the collection of salt.

Lake Retba, Senegal's Pink Lake

Here, as the lake at its deepest is only as high as an average adult's knees, men row to a favourite spot on the lake and dig up the salt. After filling up their buckets with salt, the men take the heavy buckets to shore where the women bag the salt. There are over 600 men and 400 women who engage in this work every day. In a seven-hour day, a good worker can fill up 12 buckets, earning the equivalent of $0.50 per bucket.

The bags of salt are piled up around the lake. Once the salt has been bagged, large trucks come and collect the bags and transport them to the city. There is no processing on site as was the case in both Peru and Bolivia. The salt is sorted according to the two established grades. One is food grade, which means the salt can be consumed mainly in West Africa; the second grade of salt means it is to be exported to France, where it is used to salt the highways during winter.

Also at the lake was an indigenous village. Again, I was not aware of it and so I was not expecting anything. The driver/guide took me to the village and the chief came out to meet me. He walked me around and then took me into their craft shop to offer me some of their goods for purchase. I declined as politely as possible. Undeterred, the chief asked me to make a donation to the village. Again, I declined.

Some of the houses in the village are thatched, while some are made of modern-day concrete. I believed that while the villagers have earned enough money to be able to live in the more comfortable concrete houses, they keep the traditional thatched houses just to show the tourists! They also have a well from which they draw water. I wondered what the water tastes like as on one side was the Pink Lake and on the other, the Atlantic Ocean.

I was happy to visit and explore the village but I was quite unhappy with the constant requests for money. The hour-long tour was far more expensive than I had anticipated so adding it to your itinerary is at your option.

The Village at the Pink Lake

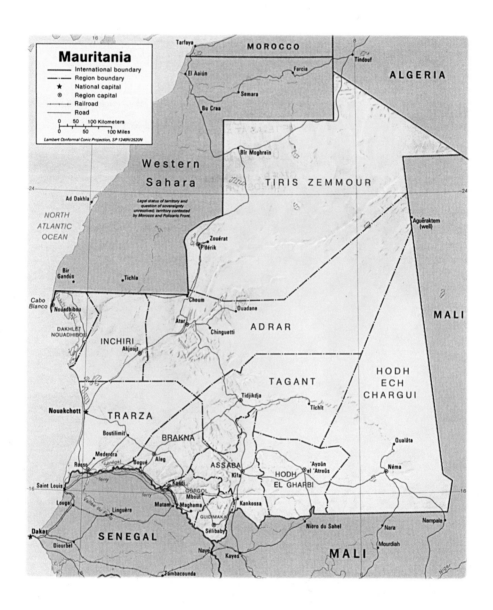

CHAPTER 2
MAURITANIA

VERY FEW TOURISTS go to Mauritania. Part of the reason for this is the very strict position taken by the government against alcohol. There are very few places in the country where an alcoholic beverage can be purchased. In addition, Mauritania only recently (in the last 10 years) made slavery illegal, yet the practice continues, just not openly.

I was very interested to go here as I found it a real challenge to my thinking that these devout Muslims could enforce in law a no-alcohol policy, yet the same officials turn a blind eye to slavery in their nation in the 21st century.

Also, I regard the northernmost countries on the continent as Mediterranean Africa, better considered as Arab Africa, whilst in the south stands Black Africa. I wanted to see within the borders of this country the two cultures in play as moving south within Mauritania the nation transforms from Arab Africa to Black Africa.

So my trip took me to the capital city, Nouakchott, as well as the desert. The capital at the time of independence was a very small town and the vast majority of its people were nomadic. Today, the shift from rural to urban has had a dramatic impact as the greater portion of the population lives in Nouakchott and other urban areas.

A Little Snag at the Border

On Friday the 6th, it was time to leave Dakar and go north to Mauritania. And boy, did I have mixed feelings! My research had thrown up as many negatives as positives. However, the most important thing was that nothing in my research made me fear for my personal safety, so all things considered, it seemed worth visiting anyway. So off I went.

The driver who had taken me to Pink Lake just the previous day promised to pick me up at 6a.m. and take me to the bus station. It turned out, he was punctual and true to his word. By 6, we were on the move. Initially in the dark, I was impressed by the number of crowded buses taking people to work along with those walking along the road.

Once at the bus station I sat back as the driver found the car I should take and then secured the front seat for me. The sept-place car is a Peugeot that can seat seven passengers. These are the long-distance workhorses. They piled our bags on the roof of the car, tied them securely in place, and off we went.

I had determined that the drive to Saint-Louis, Senegal could take from four to six hours, followed by two hours more to reach the Mauritanian border, and four hours from the border to Nouakchott, the capital of Mauritania. The mystery was how long at the border.

The driver was fast but cautious. At one point, we were very close to a minibus, and I wanted to take a picture to record how passengers travel on these vehicles. The young men at the back saw me taking their picture and signalled their disapproval. I responded by showing them the hand signal that meant, "Okay, I'll stop." That appeased them, so as we passed them, we gave each other high-fives. No need for extra drama!

The first leg of the trip took only four hours and at noon we were passing through Saint-Louis. I was very pleased. I was hoping that we would get to the border as quickly, but the vehicle was stopped by the police. They were asking for passports. I was asked to leave the car.

I was bewildered as I had no idea where I was or why my bag and I were removed. I watched helplessly as my car drove off. The police started to question me but I had no idea what was going on. A crowd of glad-handers gathered quickly. Before I knew it, I was on the back of a motorbike and the driver had my bag between his knees and we were driving to the police station.

So we were at the border. I should tell you that some have called this the most corrupt border in the world. Now I was to see for myself.

Trouble at the Police Station

I was brought to the police station. But the policeman who had my passport was not there yet. He arrived a little later, telling me to wait outside. I counted perhaps 20 minutes and then I was called in. They began asking me a couple of very routine questions, after which my passport was stamped. Great, I can go, I thought.

Actually, no. The policeman took me and my passport to another building. It was full of men who all turned their attention to me. They asked me if I had any dollars or euros. I knew from my research that it was difficult to use credit cards in these parts, so I had been carrying some amount of cash with me. They wanted to know how much I had!

Imagine the scene: A room full of men with a group of six right up to my face. They were telling me that Mauritanians will take this money from me so I must have my cash converted to local currency with them. Can you believe a policeman had taken me to this room! So very reluctantly I told them how much cash I had with me. They began asking me to show it to them, offering to change it at a really lousy rate. I refused. So one of them said, "You HAVE to change it with us as WE are the black market!"

I countered with a better rate, which they refused. So I loudly said it was my money and I would take it across and give it to the Mauritanians. That changed everything. Now they offered to change at least $100 so that I will have some Mauritanian money when I cross the border. This was like a scene from a movie. I could not believe it.

So I changed the $100 at a satisfactory rate and now left with my passport and a smaller band of helpers.

I went down to the water to cross into Mauritania. Boats were used to cross the water, with boys swimming in the water with their horses.

There was a lady in green ahead of me who dipped her arm into that dirty water and wiped her forehead several times. I was still wearing a smile at this point. It was about two in the afternoon now.

We got across, with one man who had appointed himself as my guide. He brought me to another man who took my passport. He came back and told me that my appointment was at 3p.m.. Now my day was starting to go sour.

For the next 40 minutes, I stood around doing little. At close to three, I returned to this man only to be told that the appointment was now at 4p.m.. Meanwhile, there was a room next door with two immigration officers sleeping on the floor. Great.

Finally, it was 4p.m.. I got my passport examined and approved, but not stamped. I had to take it to another room where it was stamped. I now have to go to yet another room where all my stuff had to be searched and my money counted. After that, I was made to go to yet another room where a form was signed stating how much money I have.

Finally, I was let through the gates into the country.

However, my handler took me to one more man who had to see my money and sign the last form I had been given. At this point, I lost it. I started screaming (like I was in Parliament, I guess), compelling them to decide they have had enough of me and told me to go.

The last thing my handler had to do was get me a seat. I believed the fare should be UM 3000. A man offered to take me in his cab by myself for UM 15,000. A Sept driver said he would take me for UM 7000. Finally, my handler got me a seat in a sept-place cab that looked like it shouldn't be on the road for UM 3500. We set out at 5:10p.m..

Welcome to Mauritania.

Nouakchott

Having had a long and tiring day previously, I was glad to have a more relaxed one on the day that followed, a Saturday. Nouakchott, the capital city of Mauritania, had only a few historic sites. The city was only a small village of some 17,000 people at the time of the country's independence in 1960. The French had administered Mauritania from Saint-Louis in Senegal, which for many years was the capital of the French West African Empire.

The people of Mauritania had been nomads for hundreds of years and by the country's independence, it was estimated that 70 percent of the population still lived in that manner. Since 1960, people have flocked to the capital city, leaving only 23 percent of the population deemed to be nomads today. The city now has over one million people. For the country, this was a huge change in how they live and function.

I went to one of their markets and saw nothing of note. And nothing else that I saw that day took my attention.

The following day, Sunday, was my scheduled journey into the desert. I was to embark on a five-and-a-half-hour northeast trip to the desert town of Atar. I was to spend three days in the desert! Yes, I was excited.

We took a 16-seat minibus for the journey which meant we would be in close quarters for several hours. After about three hours, we reached a small desert town, where some people departed the bus, while others joined. This meant new cargo—they even loaded goats on the vehicle's roof! We then set off for the final leg of the journey.

Finally, we arrived on time in Atar at 1:30p.m., with the temperature a boiling 39° Celsius.

Atar

I arrived at the desert town of Atar. I had requested online that the hotel arrange tours for the next three days and so I was ready for my desert experience.

I got my stuff together and took a taxi to the hotel just a little out of town. When we arrived, I noticed a wire fence going across the entrance. The driver encouraged me to step over and go in before he drove off.

So in I went—only then did I find out I entered a construction site. There was on-going work everywhere. But since it was Sunday, no one was around. I looked around and saw one bed that could be slept in but....really!?

Fortunately, I arrived on the morning bus. The afternoon bus would have arrived at 10:30p.m. and that would have been a complete disaster. My decision to take the trip early was due to some wise advice given to me many years ago by a wise experienced traveller—my dad: "Always travel early as you never know what you might run into!" That advice has saved me a whole bunch of times over the years!

I walked back to the main road and started flagging cars. The third or fourth one stopped and, by a combination of spoken English words and gestures, I asked to be taken to another hotel I had researched. They dropped me at this hotel which was in town.

In I went and found it was also under renovation! Not as bad as the last one, but this hotel really should not be taking guests. Oh, dear! I walked through the whole place (it had about 10 guest rooms) and saw no one. So I crossed the street and found a man who spoke English. He assured me that the hotel was open and while we were standing in front of the hotel, a car stopped and it turned out to be the hotel's non-English-speaking owner!

He showed me around, I picked a room and we worked out an agreement for four nights at a really steep rate. But considering the situation, I had little bargaining power. He called his manager over and he got me settled.

Time was ticking away. I could not get my phone to work so I spent time trying to find someone who could fix it. I needed to book tours otherwise the trip to the desert would be a bust. As Atar is the major desert town in this part of the country, there were a lot of tour operators in town but how do I pick the right one?

Clearly, the best thing to do then was eat! And I prayed for a miracle. After eating, I used Itranslate on my cell phone to explain to the lady who ran the restaurant my situation. She immediately went across the street to a tour outfit. In a short while she returned with one of their staff who could not speak English but did get me to understand that he was calling somebody that I should talk to. Soon I was talking to a tour guide who was at that point out of town finishing a tour but would be driving back later. We made arrangements for a two-day tour for Monday and Tuesday and for me to meet him the next morning at the office at 7 a.m.. He said that he was going to arrange the sleeping so I should check out when I leave the hotel.

This is great, I thought. I got two days of tours and accommodation so now I had to find the hotel manager. Later, the manager knocked on my door. He knew about my arrangements and I paid him for the one night, agreeing to leave the keys in the room when I leave!

Came very close to disaster! Prayed my way out of this one!

Meeting Atar's Own "Tom Cruise"

Early Monday morning, I was standing at the tour office and a very personable young man greeted me. He told me his name was Abdul Tom Cruise. In reality, he was Abdul Kruze, a guide of 14 years. We went to his home so that he could change his gear from the previous trip and pull together what he needed for ours. We agreed on a visit to the old city of Chinguetti and a trip into the desert for today and a trip to the beautiful Terjit Oasis tomorrow.

With that, we set out. I found the terrain quite surprising. Along the way we stopped at a place where animal shapes from over 30,000 years ago could be seen. It was quite amazing to see these cave drawings.

Our drive to Chinguetti took just over two hours and when we got there it was at the hottest time of the day, 39°C (about 102F). Abdul took me to the home of a friend where we rested and spent the afternoon before heading out for Chinguetti and the desert.

Islam's 7th Holiest City

Once the afternoon temperature lowered, we set off to tour the city of Chinguetti. At its height, the city was a medieval Berber trading centre. It is located two hours' drive east of Atar. In 2000, UNESCO deemed this city along with three other desert cities, to be World Heritage sites.

During the 13th century, many passed through Chinguetti on their way to the pilgrimage at Mecca. However, the journey took so long that some decided to make the pilgrimage to this city and then return home. Because of this, Chinguetti has been considered the 7th holiest city of Islam.

Today, the city is under threat from the advance of the desert. On the western side, several houses have been lost to sand dunes. This will be a greater issue as time passes. The city is built in typical Berber architecture, with red stones and mud brick. Among the still standing structures are the Friday Mosque and a tall water tower.

I have been to a good many ancient sites in my travels but I believe this to be the most complete ancient city I have ever seen. In addition to viewing the city, there was a library that held manuscripts from this same time period. These books were studies in astrology, maths, science, literature, and poetry.

Enjoying Tea in Chinguetti

Mauritanians drink a lot of mint tea. The process is quite time consuming and it is somewhat of a social ritual as the maker will sit with friends who are to have the tea and they would talk and share while the tea is being made.

The young lady in these pictures is our host in Chinguetti. Soon after our arrival, the tea making started. I asked if I could take pictures and she agreed. It was pointless to make a video as this tea took well over 30 minutes to make.

In the first picture you can see the propane gas unit. This serves as the stove in desert homes and it is carried from room to room as needed. There are two kettles usually four cups and of course, water, sugar and tea bags.

In the second picture, the making of the tea is progressing. She can be seen pouring the hot tea into glasses. It is then poured back into the kettle and heated some more.

The mentioned process continued, until finally, the tea was poured from glass to glass. This was done repeatedly until the taste was to the satisfaction of the maker. She may add more water, sugar or tea depending on her taste.

When it is ready, the white foam in the glass will be three or four times the actual tea in the glass. When served, the tea was quite hot and was sipped before drinking the rest in one gulp.

It is not unusual for a person such as this lady to do this four or more times in a day.

The home we stayed at had three sisters and two young girls. Both girls went to school. The middle sister is married but her husband works in Atar so he does not come home often during the week.

The home included three rooms which could be used as bedrooms. They had no furniture, just a good carpet and cushions to recline on. I am sure that would not work in Bermuda! Additionally, there was a kitchen, storeroom and bathroom. The bathroom had a tiled hole in the ground for using the toilet. You took a bucket into the same room to bathe. I saw no mirrors.

Within the family compound the ground was sand. Despite this, the family was probably middle class as they had satellite TV.

We drank a lot of mint tea made by the married sister during our stay. For lunch, we had chicken with potatoes cut in square cubes and fried. At dinner, we had a rice dish. The meals were served on communal trays with four people sitting around the sides. After washing your hands, you ate with your right hand only. You ate as much or as little as you wished until the food was gone.

As it hardly ever rains, we slept outdoors on mats but I woke at around 2a.m. because it was cold so I went inside for the rest of the night. The sky was clear and the stars and the moon were beautiful.

Unfortunately, I had to sleep in an upright state as the floor inside was concrete covered only with the carpet/prayer mats.

As you can see, the short stay with this family was not included in my tour, but it was truly a delightful addition to my experience of the place!

The Terjit Oasis

After a good night's rest, my guide and I said goodbye to the family and headed out for the Terjit Oasis. This oasis is thought to be one of the most beautiful in the world in the rainy season when the water is high. Our drive through the desert was so stunning that I spent the four-hour drive gawking at the scenery.

The Terjit Oasis is located some two miles south from Atar. I was really excited about seeing this beautiful oasis. One could see the arid plateau, and one wonders how a small stream of water turns into a beautiful oasis. The amazing thing is that this fresh water runs very cold in some parts and warm in others. I was able to drink cold clean water that fell from the rocks to quench my thirst.

Because of the beauty of the oasis, various religious ceremonies take place here, including weddings. At the time of our visit, the water was quite low, which was a disappointment but I was able to swim in it, nonetheless. There were only a few others there but at the height of the season the crowds can get large as people seek relief from the desert heat.

Renewable Energy in Mauritania

I'm pretty sure you know how I feel about the use of renewable energy sources. My time in Mauritania had been full of adventure of one type or another. It would be easy to dismiss the country as a backward backwoods behind-the-times place and to leave it at that—except it is not entirely true.

In the main street in the desert town of Atar, I found that they are using the sun to power their street lights. Having sun every day and so little rain, they have installed solar panels to light up their streets.

In the capital city of Nouakchott, I found more implementation of solar energy as they too used solar power for their street lighting right to the outskirts where they even have windmills!

No more bad stuff to say about "backward" Mauritania.

Back in Nouakchott

Now back in Nouakchott, I spent a day doing some touring. As Mauritania is almost completely Muslim, it has a grand mosque in the centre of the city. However, I could not enter.

Later my friend, Pa Modou Sillah explained that it was nothing against me but that you cannot enter a mosque unless you wash ghusl, which is a Muslim spiritual washing of the entire body which non-Muslims do not do. He further explained that if he did not do this he could not enter.

I continued my tour by visiting the nearby National Museum of Mauritania. This two-storey museum houses both archaeological and ethnographic collections. Unfortunately, a special exhibit, which was generating much excitement, was scheduled to open on the upper level in the following week, so I was only able to view the ground floor that houses the archaeological exhibits.

For the students of history among us, the excitement is due to the fact that the special exhibit showcases the Moorish culture. There are many objects from daily life, thereby revealing how the ancient peoples lived in this land.

Of special interest to me was the display dealing with the role played by the ancient cities, including Chinguetti, the city I visited merely two days earlier.

My day of touring would not have been complete without a stop at the Marche Capital, the Capital Market, the main market of Nouakchott. It is crowded. It is chaotic. It is a very lively place. I know a lot of Bermudians would love this place. All kinds of goods are on sale here at the customer's best price. The vendor standing in front of you may first offer to sell the item for three times what he really wants for it so when he says 100 and you counter with 50 he is already ahead of the 33 he would have liked to get. What a game.

CHAPTER 3
BACK TO SENEGAL

S AINT-LOUIS, SENEGAL IS worthy of a visit by tourists who are interested in the history of French West Africa. Today, the inner island stands as a living museum of the time of French colonialism. Upon independence, the French pretty much left *en masse*, leaving the buildings in the French half to deteriorate. Contributing to further deterioration are ownership issues relating to the properties in that sector.

I had several reasons for visiting Saint-Louis. I love history and Saint-Louis provides living history. I also like the city's predominantly 19th century architecture, as well as its colourful and lively markets.

Saint-Louis

I was able to leave Mauritania and return to Senegal with far less hassle than going the other way. Once I had cleared the border I smiled to myself over the experience. When I was going into Mauritania I had to count my dollars and euros in front of three different sets of people. I had an official form recording how much of each currency I was taking into the country. It was said that upon leaving Mauritania, I would have to produce the form and account for any differences with invoices, etc. All a bit unnerving. Well, I re-entered Senegal and to date no one has asked to see the form! It was all part of the border scam.

Having returned to Senegal I went to Saint-Louis, about an hour inside the border. Under the French colonial regime, Saint-Louis was a very important coastal region as it was the administrative capital of the French West African Empire. The city includes two small islands no more than 3 kilometres long with the inner island having functioned as the administrative centre while the outer island (Guet N'Dar) has long been an incredible fishing village. Their brave men go into the strong waves and currents of the Atlantic sometimes for as many as four days in tiny colourful boats.

The Cathedral is obviously in a deplorable state.

There are several reasons I had to go to Saint-Louis. I love history and Saint-Louis provides living history. I like the architecture of the 19th century and here it is. And I love the African markets and the brilliant colourful market on the mainland side of Saint-Louis is one of the best I have seen in the region. The culture and practices of these people are certainly worthy of observation and I would encourage a visit for this reason alone.

As I mentioned, the city of Saint-Louis, Senegal got its start when French traders established a base there way back in 1659 on the outer island of Guet N'dar. Saint-Louis then served as the capital of French West Africa from the 1860s till 1954 when this responsibility moved to Dakar. From 1920 to 1957, the city was also the capital of Mauritania.

Interestingly, the northern end of the island was occupied by different businesses and Muslims. In fact, on this tiny island there are 20 mosques, including the Grand Mosque which was built by the French for the people. One thing I learnt was that Islam has been practiced in Senegal since the 11th century.

The southern end was occupied by the French and Christians. Upon independence, the French pretty much left *en masse*, leaving the buildings in the French half to deteriorate. Contributing to further deterioration are ownership issues relating to the properties in that sector.

As a result, while the island itself has fallen into decay, the south had it even worse when the French and the Christians left. The Cathedral I saw was in a deplorable state. Given that those who would attend this church have left the country the only thing left to do is to knock it down!

There are many French colonial buildings in the south. Fortunately, the former governor's residence sitting pretty much in the centre of the old city is in fine condition.

In this picture, you see a night photo of one of the famous landmarks of Saint-Louis, the Faidherbe Bridge. The bridge provides a road over the Senegal River and links the island of Saint-Louis to the African mainland. It is over 500 metres long and 11 metres wide. Designed by Gustav Eiffel, it was opened to the public in 1897. Its central span rotates to allow ships up the Senegal River. It underwent rebuilding from 2008 to 2012 as a complete replica of the original with the eight semi-circular sections built in France and then assembled on site. The bridge is named after the Governor of Senegal who was most responsible for conquering the native tribes and advancing French power in Senegal, Louis Faidherbe, who served from 1856 to 1865.

Thanks to a Bermudian friend reaching out to a friend in Gambia and that friend reaching out to his friend in Saint-Louis, I had the pleasure of having dinner with a Senegalese family in their home.

The gentleman is a young businessman who has a number of projects going on. He came to my hotel and took me to his home on the mainland. Upon arrival, he introduced me to his family. Now, here was where the challenge of language kicked in. The Senegalese have French as their national language. While I, of course, speak English. So there was the potential challenge as we would try to communicate while butchering both languages. But this was not to be as he, like many others in Senegal, does not speak French but only the local language, Wolof. So we had no chance of making this communication go easy.

His wife went out soon after and she returned with two chickens who then walked around the house. Hungry but sympathetic, I thought these needed to do all their walking as quickly as possible.

Well soon after, my new friend was sharpening his knife and then effected a halal kill. I was impressed with how swiftly his wife plucked the feathers from the two birds. We continued in our attempts to speak to each other while the dinner was cooking.

Once the food was ready a tablecloth was spread on the floor. We washed our hands and the father prayed. I should mention that since we had arrived twice he had prayers.

We sat on the floor in a circle in front of the food, which in addition to the chickens was salad, rice and beans. Like the Mauritanians, we ate with our right hand. The food was excellent. I truly enjoyed myself.

This was kindness itself. Once dinner was finished, the friend suggested through the now mutual friend in Gambia, that I leave the hotel and come to live with his family. I had to be sure that in turning down such a generous offer I did not offend. My main reason for turning down the offer was the city is so small that I could walk from end to end. If I moved to his house I would be on the mainland and would need taxis. So far I had not been in a taxi in Saint-Louis and I wanted my stay to be free from any taxi driver incidents!

Once again, God sent his angel to watch over me.

Guet N'dar

I wanted to get a close look at the outer island known as Guet N'dar Island. So one afternoon, I took a few pictures of the shoreline from Saint-Louis Island and went over.

The island is a fishing village, as evidenced by the rows of nicely painted boats (called "pirogues") on its shore. Fishing trips out into the Atlantic can last from one to four days. Deplorably, the island is a very dirty place. Goats and people live in very close proximity. The island is 2 km long and 200 m wide, yet it has a population of 27,000 people. Imagine what that looks like.

The people on this island are quite different in their approach to life from those on Saint-Louis and the mainland. Few women who are not from the island will choose to marry men from this island so there are many generations of closely family ties. The men fish and they expect their sons to crew. To accomplish this, they raise large families. Polygamy is legal in Senegal and so the norm is that the man will have as many as six children with his first wife. Then because they live in such close quarters and have to get along, the wife will guide the man to a second wife whose persona will give peace to the growing household.

The men take care of the fishing but once on shore the women take over the tasks of getting the fish ready for market. They may work as long as from 5a.m. to 9p.m.. As a result, by the time a girl is old enough for high school, she is raising her siblings while the boys of the same age are out at sea.

A serious threat to this ever-growing population is that the sea is claiming some of the land. I could see some houses with just the land side wall standing and the rest of the house crumbling into the ocean.

While at the beach I noticed many shells of different shapes sizes and colours. I picked up a few and took pictures of them.

There were more people at the beach on Sunday compared to Saturday. However, no flashy or fleshy bathing suits at all. The local ladies swam in outfits that by and large were their street clothes. But they did not go in for long if they went in. So looking up and down the sea line one saw mainly men in the water. Why this was like this I cannot explain, as I can only share my observation.

The beach itself was beautiful. During the tourist season, which typically starts on November 1, many visitors flock to the beach, but during the off season the locals have it to enjoy for themselves.

On Monday, I took a city tour with a guide from the Department of Tourism. By this time, I had already walked over the southern part of both Saint-Louis and Guet N'dar. However, it was wonderful to hear the story from this man's perspective.

There are two principal reasons for the state of the old houses in Saint-Louis. First, the original building materials were imported directly from Toulouse in France. For many years, obtaining the product from France has been prohibitively expensive. Prior to the country's independence, the French built a plant in Saint-Louis. However, the salt content was such that the final product was inferior. Thus, the amount necessary to restore to the standard required is very expensive. Second, after many years, ownership of houses would become uncertain.

Some families live in such houses for years without doing any repair because they do not have the title to the property. On the other hand, some people have totally refurbished the house that they live in only to have the "rightful" owner show up and take them to court and prove their ownership, thus forcing the person who had restored the house off the property. Where ownership can be proven these terribly damaged houses are being sold to the French, creating some dissent among the locals in Saint-Louis as this is seen as regressing back to colonialization.

When we toured Guet N'dar, the guide explained that he was from that island but never liked fishing and so he went to university and held the job he now does. He was worried because while the islanders catch the fish and prepare it for market, the large trucks representing the bulk buyers come and buy the product, setting the price on both ends of the transaction and thereby enjoying the lion's share of the fishing business. Meanwhile, the fishing community barely survives financially. He saw this as a grave danger for the future.

The last thing that he told me took me by surprise. The people of Guet N'dar are darker than those of Saint-Louis, the guide said, offering no further explanation. But he said some of the women have begun to bleach their skin to deal with this. He very discreetly showed me two such ladies.

What an interesting pair of islands. So close yet so far apart!

Sor Market

On my last day in Saint-Louis, I walked across the bridge and went to the mainland.

I spent some time at the Sor market as I was looking for a couple of items I thought I could get there. The hustle of the market was easily spotted. I found the people who work these markets most interesting as they all brought their own style to the task. This market was spread over a number of streets and by moving around the market you can find just about anything.

Finally, it was time to move on. My third week had come to an end. Each week had high and low points. In Dakar, it was Goree Island and the Pink Lake. In Mauritania, it was the desert and the old city of Chinguetti. Saint-Louis presented an old colonial town along with a curious fishing village.

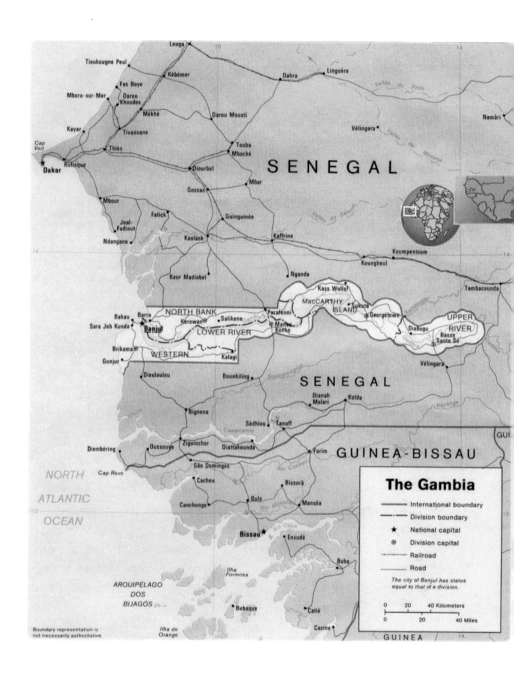

56

CHAPTER 4
THE GAMBIA

YEARS AGO WHILE vacationing in the UK, I used to see this sitcom in which one of the characters was a university student from a place he called "The Gambia." I always smiled when he said, "The Gambia." And so the Gambia registered on my mind. When I decided to start my trip to West Africa in Senegal, it was a no-brainer that I would go to the said country.

When you look at the map of Africa, you will see that the Gambia seems to have been carved out of Senegal. In 1783, the British signed a treaty with the French to give themselves a seaport and thus the Gambia was separated from Senegal. This country, the smallest in Africa, has many beautiful areas plus many nice beaches in the Serekunda area where I was to spend much of my time. It is well known in tourism circles for a certain type of tourism which aids the local economy.

This is the country to which Alex Haley was to trace his family's origins when researching for his book, *Roots*, and since the 1970s many African Americans have made pilgrimages to the Gambia to see his roots and often to search for their own.

Kaolack

Ever since I heard its name, I had been fascinated by it. But to get there, it would be on a ride in a sept-place car and it would be challenging. You will recall that these cross-country cars were available only once a day and they officially departed at 7a.m.. To avoid getting a seat from hell you had to be there early. So I arranged for the hotel to have a taxi collect me at 5:45a.m.. When the time came, I went down to the front desk only to find the night manager with his head hanging so far back that if it went any further surely it would come off! I gently woke him and asked for my cab. We then went out into the street and he sought to flag one down! After a few minutes with no success, he decided to walk from the hotel to the big bridge. If any taxi was around, surely they would pass by the bridge, he thought. He was right, as a taxi did really come and I got in.

The driver quickly took me across the bridge to the mainland and on to the station. It was 6:05a.m.. I paid my fare and was told to sit in a certain seat. The car looked pretty full. Then another person came and told me to get out of the car as I saw my bag being offloaded! Turned out someone else was ahead of me and I had his seat. So out I came!

Now as compensation I was told to take the front seat of the next car. But what compensation is this if the next car doesn't leave until noon? At 6:18a.m., I watched the first car roll out of the station 42 minutes early! I sit in car number two hoping that six other people would want to go where I was going and that they were racing to get the 7a.m. car. And of course, I thought about that sleeping night manager who had put me in this mess.

Miracle upon miracle, one by one people appear and at 6:35a.m. car number two was leaving the station. I was on my way.

For a change I had nothing to complain about: a good driver and moving quickly in a road-worthy car! Great. The next several hours passed without incident. I was heading in the direction of a town called Kaolack. It is an important town in the middle of the country. Suddenly, the driver turned to me and said "Kaolack." He then pulled up beside a similar car in a lay-by, had a quick conversation with the driver and then told me that I would continue my journey in this other car! I thought the car I was in was taking me to the Gambian border! Not so! Suppose there was no transfer car? Suppose the transfer car was full? What would happen to me? As it was, I saw my new driver speak to a young man who angrily took his bag out of the car and walked away. I realized I was given his seat.

As compensation, once more I was given the front seat. This driver was an equally good driver and we continued incident free until we came to the border. Again came the sim card salesmen selling cards that may or may not work (this time I had to buy another card two hours later when I found that the card I bought did not work); along came the money changers (the black market) and this time I got the rate I wanted (one for the good guys). And now to take the ferry across the Gambia River and I would be home and dry.

Actually not quite.

We had to take a little bus from the immigration office to the ferry terminal. As I was walking through the terminal, a female customs officer called me over and took me into her office. I opened my bag and we then proceeded to have this very awkward conversation. I did not understand why she stopped me or what she wanted me for. After a while she told me I could go. So off I went. When I sat down to wait for the ferry, a Gambian lady who had been on the bus said to me, "How much did she want?" My mouth fell open in surprise and I said, "Oh, that's what that was!" Because I was not paying attention I failed to pay her anything!

Next it was time to get in the ferry and go. The ferry ride took about 20 minutes. I was going to be picked up by someone from the place I would be staying at so that would be the end of the journey. But as I was leaving the restricted area, a man asked to see my passport. I have had enough so I aggressively responded by asking him who he was. He reached in his pocket and brought out his ID, showing him to be in the drug enforcement unit. Now we have all seen enough movies about police planting drugs in people, so I was like, oh no, not me, partner! I went for broke! I pulled out my "business card" showing I am a retired member of the Parliament from Bermuda. I told him that he can google me and he will see that I was the minister in charge of his very unit in Bermuda. Holding the card, his whole posture changed to *yes sir, no sir, three bags full, sir!* And on that happy note, I entered the Gambia. This is Africa!

Meeting Pa Modou Sillah

I had the good fortune to spend the afternoon with Pa Modou Sillah, thanks to the effort of a mutual friend, Ashfield De Vent. Some of you may remember him as a math teacher at Cedar Bridge in the early 2000s. He was a Gambian and, since his time in Bermuda, had established an NGO (Our Caravan of Mercy) in the Gambia, which has been doing marvellous work for the people.

Pa Modou Sillah and I headed north. He intended to show me two projects that he has worked on for his NGO as well as give me a feel for the area. We left the Serrekunda area at around 4p.m. and travelled until 10p.m. to reach our destination.

During the trip, we saw changes in the vegetation and as the evening progressed we could see which villages got their power from Gambian sources and which from Senegal. I found that power outages were a daily experience in the Gambia. As a result, many businesses and residences have moved to using generators and solar-powered systems. Senegal has taken advantage of its many rivers to build hydroelectric power plants and power is sold from these plants to some Gambian villages. So as we passed through an area we could tell which was which by whether power was on or not.

The next morning, we went to the two sites. The first was a school that has established a boarding section for boys in addition to classes for day students, both boys and girls. The school teaches in both Arabic and English and the students get a full slate of subjects. I was impressed with the school and with the commitment to education on behalf of these young boys. The cost of being at the school for many of the boys was shouldered by Pa Modou's NGO.

While there, I did not take any pictures of the school. This was on purpose as I did not wish to go into the boys' dorm or into classes and start taking tourist pictures.

Once we left the school, we drove to a village where Pa Modou's charity had provided the funding for building a borehole. Thanks to the borehole, which was solar powered, the village now has an assured water supply.

Pa Modou's NGO continues to need donations for their socio-civic charity works. If you would like to get involved, let me know by sending me an email to terrylister01@gmail.com.

The River Gambia

Following our visits to the two sites and getting some lunch, we went on the River Gambia in a small boat. We spent about two very enjoyable hours on the water. Our time was well rewarded as we saw some hippos playing in the water, many birds and a large chimpanzee. These freshwater hippos were too far away for me to get any good pictures and by the time we reached where we had seen them, they were gone.

We had to stop at the ranger station where we paid a fee and took a ranger into our boat. This is required if the intent is to go past the island on which the chimpanzees live.

Some 30 years ago, with permission from the government, two

American ladies brought chimpanzees from elsewhere and started a colony here on this island. Only one of the original chimps is still alive and since the passing of the ladies, the government has taken full responsibility for the chimps and the island. The rangers got on each boat to ensure the boats would not go too close to the island. And I was glad one was on mine!

As we approached the island where the chimpanzees were, there was a rustling in the trees and a large chimpanzee appeared. He was agitated and the ranger quickly directed that the boat be moved away from the shoreline as chimpanzees can not swim. He warned that if the chimpanzee reached the boat there could be serious trouble. As we pulled away the chimpanzee became more agitated and finally jumped into the water. Fortunately, we were too far away and he had to go back to shore!

Wassu

Before we left the north, we went to a place called Wassu where there were stone circles. I once had a day trip to Stonehenge and Bath. At Stonehenge, they had a nice gift shop and cafe but they don't really tell you very much about the stones. Once you pass through the gift shop you are transported to the stones where you walk around and take pictures and then head for the tour bus to go to the lovely city of Bath.

However, Wassu was very different. There was a guide who had spent the last 30 years of his life learning about the stones and sharing what he has learnt. He carefully explained the purpose of the stones and their significance. There was also a small museum, which opened in 2000 that helps tourists understand what the site was about.

At this point, I should say that this site was declared a national monument in 1995 and a World Heritage site in 2006. The stones sit on top of mounds that were the burial site of kings and chiefs. Carbon dating has shown the oldest parts to be over 1200 years. There is a legend about the site being cursed, with horrible fates awaiting anyone who disturbs it. This has left the site pretty much undisturbed through these many years.

There were 11 stone circles, each having 10 to 20 stones around six feet tall. Authorized digs on the site have found iron, weapons, knives and pottery as well as various other objects. As an indication of how widespread this practice was, hundreds of these stones were found in along the River Gambia.

Janjanbureh

Our very last stop before our return to the Banjul area was at the river-front town of Janjanbureh. Before 1995, the town was known as Georgetown, named after a British soldier. This was a key place for the movement of slaves prior to the outlawing of the slave trade by the British in 1807.

The picture above shows a slave house were slaves were assembled before being transported down the river and up the coast to Goree Island. There was a former auction house for the sale of slaves there as well.

Next, I walked about a hundred yards up the street to the Freedom Tree monument. This is a small fenced park with a large bantang tree planted as a reminder of the original Freedom tree. It is said that any slave who managed to touch the freedom tree was immediately freed.

The police have a station across the entrance to the park. While I was taking pictures, an officer came out and gave me some of the history of the monument.

FREEDOM TREE MONUMENT

OUR RICH PAST IS CELEBRATED IN A NETWORK
OF SPECIAL PLACES THAT TOGETHER TELL
THE STORIES OF THE LAND, PEOPLE AND EVENTS
THAT SHAPED THIS ISLAND COMMUNITY.
THESE SIGNIFICANT EXAMPLEs OF THE ISLAND'S
NATURAL AND CULTURAL HERITAGE REFLECT
OUR COMMUNITY VALUES, IDENTITY AND PRIDE.

The Gambian Wildlife

Earlier, I said that the effort to save the wildlife has had mixed results. In particular, I was referring to the green monkey. Soon after the park officially opened, visitors started feeding peanuts to the green monkeys. The red monkeys stay hidden well because in the time preceding the establishment of the park, people would hunt the red monkeys there. However, the green monkeys no longer hunt and forage, preferring to sit on the trail and eat their full of peanuts. The more senior people involved in the park discouraged this but the guides encouraged it so much so that there were peanut dispensers. My guide twice asked me if I wanted the peanuts. The guides like it because the visitors get excited by the closeness of the "wildlife" and tip better.

Personally, I am very much opposed to this sort of thing which is why I did not take part in it.

Next I was off to the Bijilo Forest Park, also known to many as the Bijilo Monkey Park. What makes this park so interesting is that it was set in an urban area. On three sides there was the growth of the town and on the fourth was the roaring Atlantic, which can be heard as you walk through the park. This area of some 125 acres was protected to provide the many forms of wildlife a refuge from man's advance. In my opinion, the results are quite mixed.

The forest was largely covered by rhun palms, with a number of trails which visitors can take. The one I was on was 4.5 km long, which was really nice as the forest cover kept direct sunlight off me but the distance ensured I saw many different trees and other plant life, as well as birds and butterflies. I did not see the diversity of animals that live in the forest but that was possibly due to the midday time of my visit.

Along the trail I saw forest, scrubland, and even sand dunes. Among the wildlife in the park were green monkeys, red colobus monkeys, squirrels, mongoose, and porcupines. Also present were monitor lizards and insects like fire ants, termites, and butterflies. I saw many green monkeys but no other animals. I also saw some termite mounds, and of course, many beautiful butterflies that would not stop and pose for my camera!

There were many birds. Over a hundred species have been recorded here, including hornbills, pheasants, cuckoos, eagles, and hawks.

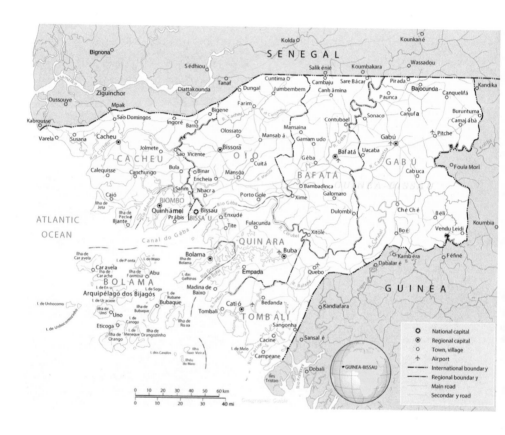

CHAPTER 5
GUINEA-BISSAU

MOVING SOUTH, MY next destination following the map was Guinea-Bissau. As a lover of history, I was a little embarrassed that I knew so little about this country. As I did my research, I found that this was a Portuguese colony and, like most such colonies, independence was achieved in 1974 at the end of a rifle. The fight for independence involved a long war that caused many deaths and involved neighbouring countries such as Guinea-Conakry.

Often called Bissau to distinguish it from Conakry, it is a small country with less than two million people with very little tourism. In 2015, for instance, there were 44,000 tourists, ranking it the 192nd most popular tourist spot in the world. Another report included Bissau as the 10th least visited country in the world. Therefore I did not expect to find a lot of tourist activities waiting for me. But there were a few historic places that caught my imagination and I thought a short time spent here would be good.

However, I was warned by my friends in the Gambia that evil spirits were very common in Bissau and that I should be on my guard! With that warning, I set out for Bissau. And I learned that the evil spirits are just myths—I lived to tell the tale!

Heros Square

After a quiet last day in the Gambia, I took a sept-place car and headed for Guinea-Bissau. As I said, I had read enough and spoke with enough people to be concerned about going to Bissau so I had my guard up the whole time I was there.

One of the people in the car with me was a Gambian man with his wife and child who was working in Bissau He decided to "keep an eye on me" when he heard me speak English. When we reached the border and had to go to the Bissau immigration, I had to buy a visa there which was pretty much standard practice.

No one in the office could (or would) speak English and so I was at sea to some degree. To be honest, I felt it was a ploy to get money out of me but I certainly did not share that thought with anyone. In a three-way exchange, my guardian angel was able to get a visa issued for me (as should have been the case) but while I "knew" the visa was 30,000 CFA francs, they required me to pay 45,000 CFA francs! And, of course, I had to smile a lot and act very pleased at the "special" price of my visa.

When we reached the city of Bissau, my guardian angel flagged a cab for me to confirm how to get to my hotel and agreed on a very reasonable charge with the taxi driver.

The Cathedral

Settled in Bissau, I went to see some of the sights the next day. The people of Guinea-Bissau are 50% Muslim, 40% follow traditional African practices, while 10% describe themselves as Christian. So the Catholic Church does not enjoy a large following here and the cathedral is the centre of Roman Catholicism in Bissau.

Over the past three years I have been to many marvellous cathedrals. However, here I was standing in front of one before I realized it was the cathedral I was looking for!

There is nothing spectacular about this 1950 building at all. It does sit on a large block in the core of the old city but that may be its only asset.

Of interest to some is the fact that the church also serves as a lighthouse having a green light at the top of the building that guides ships into the Port of Guinea-Bissau.

Presidential Palace

Apart from the cathedral, I visited (not true! I saw) the Presidential Palace. I may be wrong, but I think there has not been an orderly transition from one administration to the next since Guinea-Bissau won its independence from Portugal in 1974. Furthermore, during the 1998/99 Civil War, the palace was very badly damaged to the point that it could not be occupied.

Against this recent history, there are no tours and people are not allowed to wander into the heavily guarded grounds. The taking of pictures is not encouraged so I took the one picture and was satisfied to walk on.

The building is the official residence of the president. Having been destroyed in the Civil War, it was rebuilt with Chinese financing and reopened in 2013 some 14 years after it had been destroyed. The cost to one of the poorest nations in Africa was USD 8 million.

Next, I wanted to see the Museum of African Artefacts. I had read several articles about the museum but could not find an address for it! Quite amazing. But as an indication of how not ready for tourism this place is, I went to the front desk of my very modern hotel and asked where I would find it. The two very nice ladies at the desk admitted that they did not know. So they called the manager who came out and started to explain but then stopped and said, "Follow me." We went out of the hotel and he pointed to the structure that was just two buildings away from where we stood! The truth!

This very small museum is the guardian of the cultural history and the arts of Bissau. The many cultural pieces include pottery, weaving, and sculpture.

The building that houses the museum is part of the city university. For some reason, the number of visitors is very low. When the curator realised I wanted to come in he opened the locked door and took me by the hand and quickly walked me through the rooms, giving me an overview of what was there. It seemed as if I may have been his first visitor for the day....or maybe the week!

The pictures above are of Bissau Velho or old Bissau, showing the Portuguese architecture of an age past. Tourists are encouraged to visit the area, although they are also warned that many buildings are in need of repair work.

I walked around the area and was quite disappointed by the state of the buildings. Clearly, few people have any interest or pride in the area. Some of these buildings would start to look marvellous with just a coat of paint!

As you can see, many of the buildings are run down. And walking through the area made me very uncomfortable. I did not feel safe at all and it was 2p.m.! Safety would be one of the many reasons why this place cannot be regarded as ready for tourism.

Fortaleza de Sao Jose de Amura

Today, I wanted to get a good look at this old fort built by the Portuguese in the 16th century. The fort was designed to provide defence from any attack from the sea by other European powers as this country was the only foothold that Portugal had in West Africa. It was also to defend from land attack by the various African tribes back in those days when the Portuguese controlled only a few miles inland.

When I arrived I was expecting to see something similar to either Fort Scaur or Fort St. Catherine's at home in Bermuda. I was surprised to find a working fort. Today, it is a military base. I asked if I could go in and was refused entry. Then I was told it was possible the following day, then after some calm, gentle persuasion, I was told I could go in.

Once inside, two older gentlemen—more than likely officers but non-English-speaking—gave me a tour of the renovated portion of the fort. There was a board with before-and-after pictures, which showed the massive change that had recently been made. The official opening of the renovated area was 24th September 2017. Included in the new facilities was a lecture hall, several classrooms, and a museum dedicated to the battle to liberate the nation.

I wanted to take pictures but knowing Guinea-Bissau's post-liberation history, I did not even attempt to take one. To be honest, I was surprised that they were willing to show me so much not knowing if I was really a tourist.

One exhibit featured the rebuilt car of the hero of independence, Amilcar Cabral, who was targeted for assassination by the Portuguese. He was killed in his car in Conakry, Guinea in January 1973. He is buried on the grounds of the fort although I was not shown the exact spot.

My hope for Guinea-Bissau is that internal conflict, civil war and widespread corruption become a thing of the past and the country and its people can soon enjoy the promise of independence that they had fought for.

The Fortress in Cacheu

Cacheu is a small village further up the coastline from Bissau. It was the first place where Europeans made transatlantic slavery a big business. It is thought that over 5 million Africans were sent to Brazil from this tiny fortress. While it was the capital of the Guinea-Bissau colony from the 16th to the 19th centuries, today there are only 10,000 people who live in the vicinity.

Near the fortress is a very nicely renovated building that serves as the museum that opened last year, commemorating the history of the slave trade in the country. Quite fittingly, it's the same building that served as the headquarters of the Portuguese firm that traded in valuable cargo that, of course, included Africans destined to the New World.

I was determined that I would take a bus for the two-hour trek to the fortress and museum. My interest was sparked by reading that Drake and Hawkins had raided the fortress in 1567 and stolen those bound for the New World and had taken them to sell themselves. You see, I was a Tudors and Stuarts man! I did my history GCE covering this period of British history. Back in the day I could tell you almost anything about the Tudors, in particular. Drake and Hawkins were among my heroes. Imagine my absolute shock about ten years later when I learned that these two heroes of mine were also slavers! My history classes had not taught me that! I developed a new under-standing of the word "his story"! So when I read that these old heroes of mine had done the dirty on the Portuguese at Cacheu, I had to go!

When I found the fortress, I was surprised by its size. It was very small. I had thought the slaves were kept in a large fortress prior to transport when it appeared that they were kept elsewhere and brought to the fortress only when the ship taking them arrived and was ready to leave. Rather than a door of no return, here there was a bridge of no return. Parts of the bridge can still be seen but there does not appear to be any intent to restore it. I could not go into the fortress as there was only one man who was trusted with the key and this fine gentleman had decided to go to Bissau that day! So here I was at Cacheu and he was in Bissau! Without the key, I could look into the fortress and was sadly disappointed to see it overgrown with weeds. I wandered around and took some pictures but I did not have a positive feeling about my trip to the fortress.

The museum, as stated already, is fairly new. It is a very attractive building and has large windows to let the light shine in. Thankfully, I could look in through these windows and see some interesting displays. Once again, only one man could be trusted with the key. And he, too, was away from the village on the occasion of my visit. Sounds like I should have made an appointment.

From what I saw, I believe the combination of fort and museum is worthy of the two-hour journey, but only if you get to tour them! I had read an article that said the village elders believed the museum would put the village on the tourist map. Sadly, it turned out to be just another example of why Bissau should be given a miss until they understand what tourism is all about!

From Bissau to Koundara, Guinea Conakry

On my departure day from Bissau, I got up early and had to collect my clean clothes from the laundry a few blocks away and then get my visa for Guinea Conakry and passport from the Guinea Embassy that was located very close to the hotel.

Soon I was ready to leave and I was looking for a cab out front. Yesterday, I got picked up in front of the hotel and taken to the very same garage where I was going today. So I know the route.

Yesterday, the driver charged me 500 CFA francs, which was about 85 cents. Today, the driver took me on a tour! When I finally challenged him, it turned out he can speak excellent English and can "justify" his actions. When we got to the garage, he charged me 1,000 CFA francs. No surprise. It's ok. Pay and move out!

But it was not over. I was quite excited about this journey as I would be on a large USA-style bus instead of being jammed into a small car as had been the case for many times so far. Well, because he had used up a lot of time driving me around that the only such bus for the day had left!

Moreover, because of the delay, I ended up being the seventh person who bought a seat in the car going to Gabu. When the car was loaded I was in the back corner seat from hell. I could not get my feet under the seat in front of me, just my toes and a little more. I could not sit up straight as my head would constantly hit the roof! It was horrible with my body parts in pain rotation. First, my feet, then my back, then my neck, then my head. It was awful. Three hours non-stop. I did not know how I survived.

Finally, we were there. Everyone got out.

I actually did not know where to go when a young man approached me with a trolley and offered to take my bag. I explained where I was going and off we went to the garage. When we got there, we learned that I was too late for the direct car to my destination, Koundara – a town just across the Guinea Conakry border. So instead, I had to take a bus to a small village at the border then a moto taxi to the next village, then a bus to my destination. At this point, it was around 2p.m., so no big deal...except the bus was not supposed to leave until 3p.m.. It was bad enough that we were now travelling on horrid roads. It was like driving through the tracks at home after the government forgot to repave for 50 years! To make matters worse, the bus would stop for anything. Early on we passed by a group of men who had a side of beef hanging from a tree. The driver stopped and encouraged people to get off and buy some!

Eventually, we reached the border. The immigration officials were fine but I had to go to customs where the officer did not look into my bag but invited me to give him a personal donation. I did. Next, I had to stop at the police where another donation was asked for and given!

After all these shenanigans, I was finally able to cross the border and move on. So far, my journey had involved three vehicles and had costed me 7,500 CFA francs, which is about $14. I tried to get a moto and was told the price was 9,000 CFA francs just to reach the next town 12 km away!

No way.

So now I had a circle around me—sounds familiar—all telling me this was the price in French, to which I responded with "No" in English. I had to be careful how hard I pushed because eventually the border would close and everyone would go home and I might be left standing there in the dark, so pushing too hard would not be smart. They appealed to one guy who had just come over. He then turned to his driver and said he was a really good guy and that he would take me all the way to the place I wanted to reach, a trip with a distance of 36 km. Good.

He said 5,000 CFA francs was fair. I agreed to this. So I was on my way again, this time on the back of the moto taxi!

We drove the first kilometre and then had to report to the Guinea Conakry Immigration. The process was fine but before we could leave the bike had a problem and the driver decided to change the back wheel.

Once this was done we were on our way, travelling 36 km over a road that was not a road. Ruts, gullies and holes were the order of the day. I felt like a participant in an extreme sports event. But we survived and got safely to my destination. Another day of prayer! Another day where the outcome hardly resembled the plan for the day! But thank God I was where I set out to be with no harm or danger.

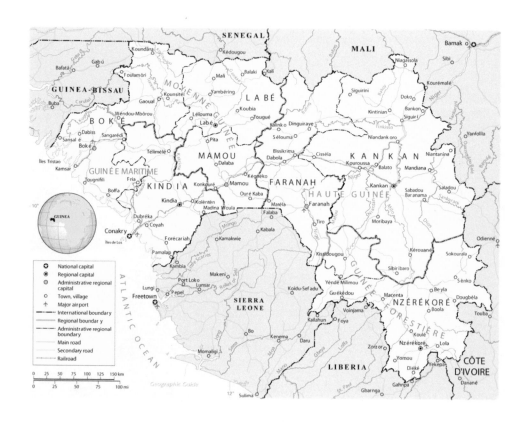

CHAPTER 6
GUINEA CONAKRY

THIS FORMER FRENCH colony is one of the largest countries in West Africa. It is roughly the size of the UK. This being so I knew I could not do it justice in a one-week stay. I had to decide to do something that would stand out so apart from the almost mandatory visit to the capital, I chose to go to the mountainous region of Fouta Djallon.

Conakry runs as far south as Ivory Coast, passing Sierra Leone and Liberia in the process. It has a population of 13 million people with income levels higher than most of the surrounding nations. It generates its income firstly from agriculture and secondly from mining, holding the title of the world's second largest producer of bauxite.

The climate can only be described as favourable throughout the year in most parts of the country but it is particularly good in the mountainous region. I went to Labe to enjoy the hills, the beauty of the countryside and, most importantly, the waterfalls. I love waterfalls. I have seen Niagara, Victoria Falls and Iguazu Falls. So I know waterfalls. The time I spent looking at the waterfalls of Conakry was absolutely delightful! Go and see for yourselves!

On November 1st, I travelled in Guinea from Koundara to Labe. As the crow flies, it was 170 km or 106 miles south but driving distance was 254 km. Supposedly, it can be done in four hours.

So I was up and at the place where the car was to leave at 6a.m.. And yes, they use the sept-place cars in Guinea Conakry as well. This country is officially Guinea but to distinguish it from Guinea-Bissau it is often referred to as Guinea-Conakry. In all four of the countries that I have been to on this trip, I found they use Peugeot cars as sept-place vehicles packing seven people in. However, in Guinea, these same vehicles are not full until they have nine live adults squeezed in! Knowing this, I really wanted to be the first person there. I was successful. I paid for the first seat—the front seat. It was still dark at this point. Can you imagine!

Having gotten my seat, I bought a breakfast of some yellowish beans in a liquid and waited, and waited. Finally, the nine places were sold at 10a.m. and we took off. You may be wondering where the extra two were sitting. One extra in the second row and one extra in the front seat! Yes, I was sharing the front seat with another grown man!

So the first 70 km went along quickly on a beautifully paved road. While driving, we passed by a burned-out gas truck in a side ditch as well as an overturned tractor trailer. Just reminders that care is required but not always taken. The gas truck accident happened days or weeks ago, but the overturned tractor trailer had happened within the last hour. Very sobering.

We were driving through the mountains and it was absolutely stunning. However nothing was perfect. The car started to overheat and the driver stopped and, in a scene I was now quite familiar with, he raised the hood and poured water all over the engine! We started again and suddenly we were the slow car. Whilst traffic was relatively light we were being passed by what little traffic there was. Inevitably, we got a flat tire. The passengers got out and watched the driver and volunteers change the tire, taking forever to do so. I could not determine the state of the spare tire that was put on, but when we started this time the slow car became the hardly moving car. I started to think that I could get out and jog alongside the car for my own fitness exercise.

Then, just for the fun of it, the beautiful highway ended and we were now driving through dirt roads. On one stretch, seeing the distance markers as we crawled along, we covered 20 km in over an hour. Finally, we entered a village where there was a shop that changed and repaired tires so he stopped and got the flat tire fixed. I smiled to myself thinking of the small amount of time I usually spend at Island Construction having my tires changed while watching this operation using equipment my dad would have used in the 1960s.

Of course, getting the tire fixed made sense but it was at a cost of us standing around while time ticked away. I was starting to get annoyed.

Finally, the tire was fixed and off we went, eventually reaching Labe. I get to my hotel just after 5 having started at 10 am. It has taken seven hours to cover 254 km which is 36 km per hour! Another day. Another adventure. This is Africa.

Labe

Now in Labe, I had to sort out some money, book my tours and get a haircut. I went to the ATM and got what I thought would be a reasonable sum of money but ended up with a large number of notes. It was amazing how many notes you could have amounting to a tiny sum of money.

I then went to get my tours booked.

I arranged to go out for four days on the back of a motor taxi. My tours would involve some trekking but would mainly cover waterfalls and outlooks.

I visited the Grande Marche in which all sorts of products were sold. I still can't get used to meat and fish sitting in 90-degree-plus temperature waiting for a purchaser. I found a barbershop and did my very best to explain what I wanted. The barber nodded his agreement and then proceeded to make two long cuts down the middle of my head that left not a blade of hair! I was done for. No way to recover from this! By the time he was finished I had been transported through time back to standard 3 at Southampton Glebe School. I looked in the mirror and there was eight-year-old Terry staring back at me!

Fouta Djallon

The next morning, I met my driver/guide at 7:30a.m. and we set off on a 30-mile ride to the first waterfall, Saala near the village of Diari. We were touring in the region known as Fouta Djallon. This is a particularly beautiful area of West Africa and it was a joy to ride in the open air each day seeing the landscape.

Saala was quite spectacular. After taking a few pictures, we rode upstream of the falls and I swam in the waters that gathered to go over the waterfall. It was very nice.

Along the journey, we kept an eye out for wildlife and saw a total of six playful monkeys. Unfortunately they moved too quickly to give me the chance to take pictures.

Day 2. Today, we drove through the most beautiful countryside you would want to see. Of the five countries I went to on this trip, this was the only area where the land rises up above sea level to any real height.

We had a very long ride to an outlook point known as *Les Echelles en lianes de Djiakan*. Or in English, "The lianes ladders of Djiakan." By the time we reached it, my bottom was quite sore from going over some very rough roads. We left the main road about 40% of the way into our journey. My driver was very considerate and tried to minimize the wear and tear but how can you avoid taking a beating if you were driving over dirt roads for miles?

When we got to the outlook point, there was the small requirement that we go down a 30-foot ladder made from sticks bound together.

Took me all of about ten seconds to decide that I would not be going down! A young lady had joined us while we were walking to this point as she was from the area and knew her way. Actually, she took a liking to my guide, asking me a lot of questions about him and later asked for his phone number! So the driver said he would go down and he took my phone to get some pictures for me. Well, once he got down the first ladder he found an equally long second one. And yes, I was happy that I was still at the top!

While we waited for him, a young boy looking to be 8 to 10 came and went straight down, then three teenage girls came and spoke with the young lady for a while and then they started down. And in the manner of young people, they played around, trying to pull each other off the ladder!

When my guide returned, he showed me his pictures and explained what I was witnessing. At the lower level, there were three villages. In order for the people to come and go in this direction, they must climb the ladders. I was told that women with their babies tied to their backs climb the ladder and men go down with bundles of goods that they have gone to get. I saw no evidence of a pulley system.

So that I would be able to see what he saw, the guide then walked me to another location where I could look out over the lower area. Indeed, it was such a sight.

Lastly, as we walked back to the bike which by now was some ways away, we passed by rice fields.

Of course, by this time we were very hungry so when we reached the first village we stopped to eat my most dreaded food—rice! We had a plate of rice with some mystery meat covered with sauce. All for the equivalent of USD 1.

November 5th, my son James's birthday. I get to spend the day at two more spectacular waterfalls. The first is West Africa's largest waterfall, Ditin Falls. By now, you should know that along with my thing for volcanos, I have a thing for waterfalls. All you have to do is whisper across the other side of the room is a volcano or waterfall and you have my full attention!

After the usual long ride mostly on good roads, we had to leave the bike and hike about half a mile to get to Ditin Falls. I knew something special lay ahead but...wow! My guide had laid out our four days so that after being totally blown away by the great falls yesterday, today's was even better. That was the case today.

Ditin Falls is 80-m tall with a spectacular plunge from a large plateau. We viewed the fall from two different spots which required a second quarter mile hike through the trees.

After seeing Ditin Falls in Pita in the morning of the third day, we headed off to Kinkan Falls for our afternoon trip. As always, we started on the main road and the travel was easy. But there are no falls on the main road! So soon enough we were on the dirt roads fighting to keep the bike upright.

We had last passed a village maybe twenty minutes earlier when Abdou stopped the bike and I got off to see that we had a flat tire! A crisis. He looked at the tire, parked the bike and went to sit under a large tree. He then opened his bag, pulled out a pineapple and cut it up. Crisis management. We sat off under the tree and ate the pineapple! After relaxing for a while, he told me to wait here and he climbed on the bike putting his weight on the tank and off he went to get the tire fixed. I'm really beginning to like this guy.

Now I had been travelling with him for three days so although I was in the middle of nowhere I felt no fear as I trusted him to not leave me in any danger. It was more than an hour before he returned. During that time a few people walking to their homes, I assumed, passed by and said a friendly hello.

When Abdou returned, we rode off to Kinkan Falls. What I did not know was that there was a military road block prohibiting entry without prior permission. So we rode up to this barrier and found two soldiers relaxing. Abdou explained that we wish to see the falls, speaking in Wolof so I did not actually know what was being said. After a while, one officer turned his attention to me and asked to see my passport. He was looking for my visa, which was there and in order. He then confirmed that we cannot enter. I was very disappointed but I had to accept their ruling.

Thus far, Abdou had been a really cool guy with a calm spirit as witnessed by his reaction to the flat tire. However, suddenly I saw a different person. He decided to go toe to toe with the soldiers. I start to get more than a little worried. I wanted to tell him not to bother and for us to go. But it was hot! So I stayed out of it.

Suddenly, one of the soldiers got up and lifted the barrier and told us to go through. I was shocked. We rode through and no mention was made of the incident.

So we rode to the falls. First, we saw a trickle of water running by but soon after we came to the beautiful 80-metre fall. This is a single cascade in what is known as Kinkan Canyon. I was so glad that Abdou fought to get past the barrier.

The next day I had to know what happened. So I asked. Abdou smiled and said the soldier said we were from the same tribe, who are you? Abdou responded by telling him his name. The soldier said that he had a really good friend with that surname, did you know him? Abdou said he was my big brother! The soldier told us to go through! The world is still who you know or who knows you.

Oh, he also said the soldiers wanted me to pay them before they would let me see the falls and he refused to even ask me for the money!

Day 4, our final day on the trail together. This day, we were going to see another spectacular waterfall. First, we had to ride a good distance to a small village called Ainguel. I don't really like peering at people as you pass through their homes so trips to "ethnic" sites don't appeal to me. However, in this case, this was the route to the waterfalls so I'm sure these folks were used to people tramping through their village. On top of that, folks knew my guide and were very friendly towards him. Despite this, I took no pictures and did not "bother" anyone with questions or requests.

By this time, we were deep in the jungle. However, once we walked through the village we still had about a 75-minute trek to reach the waterfalls. These falls, known as Kambadaga Falls, are 249 m tall and

69 m wide. Very large. It is a very beautiful sight with three major cascades and many smaller ones at different places.

As it started to rain, the trek back took only 60 minutes. It was the first time the rain caught me on a trip. But even so, we had a lovely landscape to look at and absorb. It was hard to balance the desire to beat the rain against drinking in the scenery.

This area that I had travelled in over the past four days is known as the Fouta Djallon. There is a comfortable climate, which is a relief from the heat on the coast and in the lowlands. There are exceptional landscapes. Beautiful waterfalls along with natural swimming pools to enjoy. Tremendous rock formations as well as spectacular granite cliffs. As I travelled, I went through traditional villages, waterfalls and rivers. This part of my West Africa trip was the most enjoyable part.

A Million Francs

This is what 200,000 looks like in Guinea. At the end of my tour within 15 minutes I paid over 1,000,000 CFA francs—straight out of my pocket. I paid the tour company the balance of the cost of four days of touring (500,000 CFA francs) then I gave the hotel manager (500,000 CFA francs) towards my final hotel bill.

Now before you dash down the path of "Terry must be loaded," let me add that this 1 million in my pocket was 1 million CFA francs which converts to USD112. I could not fold my wallet over carrying that million, but it was only USD112. I had to go back to the ATM so that I could give the hotel the remaining 900,000 CFA francs for my five nights and to have funds for my travel to the coast of Conakry.

Oh, by the way, the exchange rate at the time of writing this was USD1 = 9,029 CFA francs.

Conakry

Morning mist. I was on my way to Conakry, the capital city on the coast. I had to get to the station at 6a.m. to guarantee front seat. Again, following my dad's advice and moving early. In this car, two passengers were in the front seat. I had that experience on my trip from Koundara to Labe. It was not comfortable at all. As there were nine seats, I bought both front seats, which gave me some comfort. As we prepared to go, I heard what sounded like complaining behind me but I ignored it. The complainers should have had my dad's advice.

I have a knack for travelling with the slowest drivers. I sat quietly as one, two, three other sept-place cars steamed past us. I also have a knack for being in unfit vehicles... Actually, it's almost impossible to avoid this. In my five-country journey, only the Gambia has a fleet of taxis that looked road worthy. Next to that would be the impressive fleet of moto taxis in Labe. I would trust my life with those guys...in fact, that was what I did for the last six days and enjoyed every minute of it.

We got going. I could not believe that we left before the imaginary departure time of 7a.m.. You will recall my last journey from Koundara to Labe saw me get to the garage at 6 and the 7a.m. car left at 10a.m.. For two hours all was well. Then the driver felt his back driver's side wheel wobbling. This needed repair so he now was creeping along for two hours before he found a place where the repair work can be done. This took an hour. So by noon we have had two decent hours of driving followed by two very slow hours of driving followed by an hour of wheel repair work. That's what was going on in the above picture...and the hood was up for good measure to allow the engine to cool down.

As it was shaping up to be a really long day, we stopped for lunch at one so another hour of no forward movement. However, after lunch all was well and we got three hours of good driving...until we reached a military checkpoint where I was asked for my passport.

What gave me away, you may ask?

Usually it's the foreigners who buy the whole front seat so the military officer guessed that that's what I was. So I gave him my passport. He looked at it and invited me to follow him to a more senior officer. Hmm. The senior officer got through my passport and missed my visa. The game was on. He accused me of not having a visa. I gave him a smile and asked for the passport and turned to the page with the visa. He examined it and told me to go! My money stayed in my pocket where it belonged. Another day, another shakedown avoided!

The rainy season was over but out of nowhere the heavens open up at around five. As the journey went on, day turned into night. Another test of my patience. I did have some moments when I could have failed the test but what would I have gained? So my growth in being a more patient and tolerant person continues....and, yes, this is Africa.

Reaching Conakry from Labe was a journey of 190 miles. I left my Labe hotel at 6:15a.m. and walked into my Conakry hotel at 7:57p.m.. Fourteen hours to cover 190 miles. Now you see why I bought the front seat.

On my first day in Conakry, the capital of Guinea Conakry, formerly French Guinea, I went out to a number of very interesting sites, the most interesting of which was the Centre d'Arts de Acrobatiques.

I went to the national sports stadium where I found high school football and basketball tournaments in full swing. As interesting as these appeared to be, they were not what I was looking for. So I asked where I would find the acrobatiques. I had read about this group of young performers and decided to attend one of their daily training sessions.

They train in a gym at the national stadium called the Keita Fodesa Acrobatic Art Centre. Mr. Fodesa had a vision for young people and has established this place to train street children in circus arts. These students were given a daily meal and literacy classes to help prepare them for life. The school helps the students with artistic training, professional training and with support for schooling. As the students grow older, those who demonstrate superior skills and attitude are given the opportunity to become trainers.

The students were incredible from the half hour of very strenuous warm-up exercises to the dance routines. They worked in two groups: the boys led by a young man and the girls led by an albino young man and a young lady. Following an hour of dance they then started their acrobatic routines.

It was a treat to watch these young people and knowing their circumstances made it all the more enjoyable to watch. Even in these very difficult conditions, young people can be given opportunity by committed adults who want to see them achieve.

After watching the young people, I went to see the Grand Mosque of Conakry. Of course, not being Muslim, I could not go in but I was able to take a couple of photos.

This mosque is the largest in West Africa and the fourth largest in Africa. It was built in 1982 with the bulk of the funding being provided by Saudi Arabia. The mosque can accommodate 2,500 women on its upper level and 10, 000 men on its lower level.

The building has four slender minarets which can be seen in the picture above, as well as four domes surrounding a larger dome. The grounds have a mausoleum which has the tombs of three national heroes: Guinean Muslim cleric Samari Ture, first president Sekou Toure and 19th century ruler of Labe, Alfa Yaya.

The last thing I did on my first of two days in Conakry, Guinea was to visit the Monument du 22 Novembre 70. You will recall from my stories on Guinea-Bissau that the battle for independence from Portugal for the people of Portuguese Guinea (Guinea-Bissau) lasted from 1963 to 1974. There was much support for the rebel fighters in Guinea Conakry as well as other places. By 1970, the leader of the independence movement, Amilcar Cabral, was running the operation from Conakry.

The Portuguese wanted Cabral badly so on November 22, 1970, Portuguese troops along with some African Portuguese launched an invasion of Conakry. The operation was named Operation Green Sea and the objective was to free Portuguese troops held prisoner in Conakry's most notorious prison, destroy as many of the rebel ships as possible, and to capture both Cabral and the President of Guinea Conakry, Sekou Toure.

These troops came on land from four unmarked ships which had sailed from Portuguese Guinea. They succeeded in capturing the prison and setting free the 26 Portuguese troops being held there. However, the coup attempt failed as they could not find either of the two men they were seeking. They did destroy some ships and the air force infrastructure. They then retreated to Portuguese Guinea.

The attack was roundly condemned by the UN and the OAU. However, it did not stop Portugal from attempting to keep its West African colony. Independence was not achieved until 1974 by which time Cabral had been dead for 8 months having been murdered in Conakry in 1973.

The monument is to those who lost their lives fighting the invaders. It was officially opened on November 22, 1971 by President Toure.

CHAPTER 7
SOUTH SENEGAL

Having enjoyed my time in Guinea-Conakry, I had to fly back to Dakar then on to colonial Ziguinchor, the largest city in the Casamance region.

I was able to enjoy the Casamance River and the beach town of Cap Skirring. These were both delightful places worthy of a visit, with Cap Skirring regarded as having the most beautiful stretch of beach in West Africa. Read on!

In leaving Conakry, I flew to Dakar, Senegal for a couple of days before heading to the

Casamance in south Senegal.

Ngor Island

My first stop was Dakar. On my first day, I went to Ngor Island. This is a very small island off of Dakar, in fact, it is the westernmost point of Africa.

The island is 800 m long and 200 m wide. It has three nice beaches on the bay side and a few restaurants. To get there, one must go across in a pirogue, which runs every 20 minutes. The distance across is around 400 m so it takes no more than 10 minutes but only the very lucky manage to get across without pants and shoes getting very wet! Many people, both tourists and locals, go across as it is a good getaway from the city.

There was good swimming on the bay side and the water was clean. I was hunting for sea shells but did not find any on the beaches there.

I spent about an hour walking around the island. On the Atlantic side it was very rocky. But the island itself was quite interesting with many artsy buildings as well as a military site, which possibly covered about 20% of the island's land mass. I took a look at some of the art galleries and talked with some of the vendors before purchasing a wooden carved mask.

Overall, it was a day well spent, very relaxing after the hard riding every day in the Labe region!

Ziguinchor, Casamance

On Saturday, I flew to Ziguinchor, Casamance. On the map, you will see that the Casamance is on the "other side" of the Gambia. This has led to problems for the region.

Whereas many parts of Senegal are dry, the Casamance gets plenty rainfall leading to great forests and the production of large quantities of rice. Driving through the roads, one sees many rice paddies as the culti- vation of rice is the leading economic contributor to the region. More importantly, while the majority of Senegal's population are from the Wolof tribe, the people of this region are Djolas. Thus, they practice different customs and beliefs. These differences, along with others, have resulted in Africa's longest-running civil war.

Since the 1980s, separatists in the Casamance have been involved in armed skirmishes for independence from Senegal. The unrest would appear to die then would flare up again. By the time I decided to go in the late fall of 2017, the area appeared to be peaceful, so happily I went.

The night before I was to fly out, I ate in an Indian restaurant and during the night I became sick from the food. Great!

My flight was at 8a.m. and I was at the airport at 6:45a.m. feeling quite sick. I had a good flight and as soon as I got to my hotel I went to bed. Later, I got up to get lunch and then I took a look at the town. Ziguinchor has a reputation for having old colonial buildings. Sadly, what I saw were many old buildings in a sad state of disrepair. The quaintness of the place was destroyed by this general sense of decay.

I wanted to have a river trip so I arranged one for Sunday through the hotel. We had a 9a.m. start with a non-English-speaking guide and two of us tourists. I was joined by a young man from Switzerland who at 25 was a world traveller himself. Starting out we saw a sunken ship now used to encourage fish, then we saw traps set for large shrimp.

Next came the highlight of the day as the guide spotted dolphins. Unlike the hippos that I had seen on the River Gambia that disappeared as we got close, the dolphins allowed us to get very close to them as they played.

After watching the dolphins for some time, we motored close to the flocks of pink flamingos. They were very beautiful and, like the dolphins, very unconcerned about our presence.

As we continued upriver we saw many birds.

We also noticed the shoreline including the mangroves, which provide a hiding place for crocodiles as well. We did not see any crocodiles, however.

After a couple of hours on the water we docked alongside other pirogue boats and walked inland to a traditional village filled with fruit trees.

The guide told stories about the many different trees which passed until we reached a restaurant. We had passed two tour groups on their way back to their boats as we were making our way to the restaurant. In this traditional setting, we had a typical Senegalese meal that included rice and chicken—I couldn't get away from rice and chicken!

Following our meal, we walked back to our boat and then worked our way back down the river until we returned our place of departure at around 5p.m.. We had a full day with much seen and enjoyed.

Cap Skirring

After my day on the river, it was time to move to the ocean as I was heading off to Cap Skirring. I had to walk around to find an ATM that would give me money as the first two I went to did not! I had been told that there were no ATMs in Cap Skirring so I had to have enough CFA francs to get me there and then on to the Gambia. While searching, I passed by more old colonial buildings desperate for repair like the one shown in the photo above.

The staff at the hotel had been extremely good, as good as any I have experienced in a long time. I gave the cleaning lady 4000 CFA francs and she was very happy about getting this money (US $7). I went to check out and the front desk told me it was cash only. My booking had said they took credits cards and I had asked when I arrived if they took cards and was told yes. But now it was no, so back to the ATM for more cash.

Once the bill was sorted, I took a cab to the station to get a sept-place to Cap Skirring. The fare was 1700 CFA francs but a man who had carried my bag for about 20 feet would like 500 CFA francs for doing so on his own initiative, of course. I told him no. I gave the driver 2000 CFA francs and, not receiving any change, I assumed I was being charged 300 CFA francs for my bag. Soon after, another man came and asked for an additional 200 CFA francs for my bag. I refused and took my seat.

When we left I had the pleasant experience of driving the complete journey on a well-paved road. Unfortunately, the trip was only 90 minutes rather than the seven to ten hours I had endured elsewhere—maybe it would have been seven hours if the road was in the state of some of those that I had been on before. We drove along the Casamance River pretty much the whole way and, due to the lowlands, we saw many rice fields.

After settling in at the hotel, I went to the very nice beach nearby. The season was just starting so there were not a lot of tourists, neither were there many vendors. However, I was sure I would have a relaxing time here.

The next day I went into the small town of Cap Skirring. The first thing to catch my attention was the presence of ATMs. I had been assured that there were none in Cap Skirring! Actually in researching for this trip I read repeatedly that atms would only be found in major cities. That has turned out to be a historic fact only. I found machines in every town of any decent size that I went to. The constant irritant was that two hotels were the only places that took credit cards so my trip was totally cash spending.

As I walked through the town I saw much of the same as what you see in other towns in West Africa. I still can't get used to seeing the meat vendors chopping up meat and leaving it on the counter waiting for a passerby to make a purchase.

I decided to walk beyond the town and soon went off the road and headed into the jungle. I spent about ninety minutes observing the trees, flowers and many birds. I did not see anyone else but I knew I was close to the Casamence river even though I could not see it. It was nice to be in the jungle hearing the sounds of the birds as they called to each other.

CHAPTER 8
BACK TO THE GAMBIA

FTER FOUR NICE relaxing days in Cap Skirring, it was moving day again. Now heading back to Serrekunda, the Gambia. This would be my second week in the Gambia. In planning my trip, I thought I would like to see and experience the Gambia for more than one week.

Gambia is a very interesting country, struggling to bring its people into the modern age. There is a significant divide between the rural and urban sectors with a 70% poverty rate in the rural areas. The chief means of income generation is the fishing industry, agriculture in the form of groundnuts, and tourism. Unfortunately, the tourism is mainly centred on the Serrekunda area, thus not much revenue is earned outside of this area.

The Gambia has avoided bloodshed since its independence, which is to its credit when one considers how many countries have, sadly, gone that route. There is a constant shortage of electrical power throughout the country. It is not unusual to have long periods during the day when the power is out. Businesses that can afford them have generators to ensure continued supply. This was something that I found most annoying but I had no choice other than to adjust to it.

Serrekunda

I would take a sept-place car back to Ziguinchor and then to the border and then to Serrekunda. Having had a good stay in the Cap Skirring hotel, I was looking forward to a week in a nice apartment in Serrekunda.

The sept-place to Ziguinchor was incident free and very inexpensive at only USD 2. I arrived in Ziguinchor at 11:45a.m. and went directly to a bus heading for the border, again quite cheap at USD 4. The set-up of the bus was four rows across, seating five and two benches at the back where I was facing other passengers seating three. I was sitting next to a young mother who was nursing her baby. This ain't Bermuda—after a while the mother cried *Ouch!*—the baby had bitten her!

Got to the border at 2:15p.m.. No problems at any of the border stops (i.e., no one asked for any money). Passport inspected three times. Stamped out of Senegal and into the Gambia. My passport was getting quite filled now—I may need to get a new one before I leave Bermuda again.

Now I found the car to Serrekunda but I had to wait until the car was full so I had some down time. Of course, I was used to this now but that doesn't mean I like it! Having arrived at 2:15p.m., I leave at 2:45p.m., travelling quite quickly over good roads until we reached the urban areas of the Gambia where heavy traffic forced the car to move slowly forward.

Finally, I got to the apartment hotel at 5p.m.. Another day of travelling a not-too-great distance over a full day. I was developing my patience skills.

But then the fun started.

The owner said that payment was by cash up front and was unwilling to even allow me to take my bags to the apartment before paying. This was news to me. So I, suddenly feeling quite tired, trudged off to the ATM. The full amount for the week was 16,000 Gambian dalasis, which was just over us USD300 (not unreasonable at all for a lovely apartment) BUT the ATMs in the Gambia give a maximum of 3,000 dalasis in a single withdrawal, so I had to make at least six withdrawals. And, of course, the machine was on the street, subject to observation by any one passing by or, worse, standing and watching the activity at the ATM. So you know I was not happy about this at all. I make three maximum withdrawals and then my card was blocked.

Very annoyed, I stomped back to the apartment. I saw the owner and, quite irritably, explained my problem. He backed off and agreed to take money for two days and allowed me to go to the apartment. I had to call the bank to activate my card but my cell phone was dead.

So I could do nothing but wait for the battery to charge and get more annoyed. This was the third time on this trip that my card was blocked. Each time it happened, I had to give the bank my travel info and the assurance was given that this would not happen again. But it does, then the person I would be dealing with would tell me the card was not blocked! I don't believe this! Then the person would ask for my travel details, noting that there was nothing in my file! Welcome to the world of exotic travel!

The Kachikally Museum and Crocodile Pool

On my first day back in the Gambia I went to the Kachikally museum and crocodile pool. It is located in the heart of Bakau, ten miles from the capital, Banjul, in a very poor neighbourhood. The place is privately owned by one of the founding families of Banjul and major land owners. Some 800 years ago this family came into the area and found the pool. The myth is that the spirits asked them to protect the pool and to populate it with reptiles. So they put two crocodiles in the pool and those were the ancestors of the eighty or more in the pool today.

The crocodiles are in the water, around the water and up on the paths away from the pool. Most visitors come with guides who tell them the history of the pool and the crocodiles, as well as the special power of the pool. They also encourage visitors to pet the crocodiles and have their pictures taken with them.

One of the special powers of the pool is that if barren women enter the pool and bathe in it they will bear children. There must be some truth to this as women continue to do this even now. I must confess, however, that I did not see any such women myself.

Before entering the pool area, visitors go through a small museum which shows the history of the Gambia as well as its culture. Visitors learn about the tribes and their weapons, musical instruments and cooking vessels.

Once I was finished in the museum, I walked to the crocodile pool. It is a strange exhibit as it is not a very large pool with some eighty Nile crocodiles with the largest being about five metres. Many of the crocodiles lie in the sun. I am sure there were about twenty doing so when I was there.

The norm is when a small group of visitors leave the museum and walk amongst the crocodiles, their guides are there to ensure nothing happens. But I had no guide....I was on my own!

I closely followed a group leaving the museum and walked through the sunning crocs and took a few pictures while listening to their guide tell the narrative. As you should expect, I chose not to pet the crocs.

When I decided it was time to leave, I looked in the forward direction and saw two large crocs on the path and no one else moving in that direction. So I was not going in that direction. I turned around to leave by walking in the direction I had come...except that required me on my lonesome to walk past three crocs who were on either side of the path... Oh, and yeah, I was scared! Truth is I was feeling very confident - until it was time for me to leave and I did not see a path out which was not lined by crocs. Then I got nervous! I summoned up all my nerve and walked past them like they were not even there…but they were!

Banjul

The following day I decided that I should go to the capital city of Banjul as, apart from entering the country, I had not been in the city in either of the two weeks spent in the Gambia.

I took a city bus to Banjul. As I entered the city, the first thing I saw was the King Fahad Mosque. This is the largest and most important mosque in the Gambia. Its two minarets grace the skyline of the city. Built in 1988, it can accommodate 6,000 worshippers. The mosque has a blend of traditional Islamic and modern architectural elements.

I got off the bus very close to Arch 22 built in honour of the former leader Jammeh's long reign. It was completed in 2016 months before the people voted him out of office. It is a great arch over Independence Drive (the main street in the city) with a museum at the top showing the advances in the country during his rule! Both the views and the museum are worth seeing.

Following my visit to Arch 22, I headed for the National Museum, which unfortunately was under renovation. I was able to see and learn the history of the country along with the people's tools and musical instruments. The museum also collects books, colonial maps, cooking utensils, masks as well as prehistoric tools.

Lastly, I went to the Royal Albert Market. This turned out to be the least impressive market that I saw on all of the five countries I have been to on this trip. It cannot compare to the Serrekunda market 15 miles up the road. Despite this, you can find a craft market, fish market, and clothing from parts of Africa and the Far East.

The Abuko Nature Reserve

Next I went to the Abuko Nature Reserve in the small town of Abuko about half an hour away from where I was staying in Serrekunda. This was the first place in the Gambia to have been given protected status in 1916. It was officially declared a nature reserve in 1978 when it was increased to its present size of 258 acres.

This is a very beautiful forest. The forest was an amazing sight in late morning with the sun breaking through the trees as well as the various ecosystems. There are 50 types of mature tropical trees in the protected area, including oil palms and mahogany.

There are several pools, the biggest of which is the bamboo pool. A fresh water pond is home to Nile crocodiles. The pond is also stocked with tilapia fish. The crocodiles eat the fish so there is no feeding by staff and no feeding show!

There are three species of monkeys in the reserve: vervet (green), red colobus, and patas. True to their reputation, the red colobus were not seen. Also, there are many baboons. While both the green monkeys and the baboons are in caged areas, some get out and freely roam. They are not afraid of humans and so they will approach seeking food.

Many bird species can be found, as well. In fact, it is thought that as many as 290 bird species may be present in the reserve. The opportune time to see bird life is early morning, so I was too late to see the birds at their spectacular best.

A small number of African turtles are in cages at the reserve while large numbers of vultures fly about.

Among the other mammals present are ground squirrels, sun squirrels, porcupines, several snake species, including black cobra, python, and green mamba. Fortunately, I did not meet any of these snakes as I walked along the trails. However, at one point I did see some scurrying through the trees and caught sight of a monitor lizard about three feet long. It all happened too quickly for me to get a picture.

There is also a fenced area with about a dozen large hyenas. I did not realize how big they grow. The oldest was 30 years old. Babies born here are released into the wild as soon as possible. Foolishly, tourists previously were allowed into the fenced area to pet the hyenas!!! This practise has been stopped with me being unable to read or question why this change was made so it's left to one's imagination.

I was quite impressed with my visit to the nature reserve. I learnt a lot in a pleasant setting.

Finishing in Senegal
Theis

After a very good week in the Gambia, I returned to Dakar for two days before heading to Theis. This is the second largest city in Senegal with a population of over two million people. Only 75 minutes away from Dakar, my sept-place ride was definitely bearable compared to the torture I had to endure on my long haul trips in the previous weeks.

A good friend of my son, James, in the UK has a farm in Theis with a Senegalese partner. I wanted to see the farm so off I went. The small farm has three operations going. First, there is an egg production aspect. The chickens in this area produce eggs for about 18 months and then, as their production falls, they are sold privately for their flesh.

The second operation involves chickens raised for their flesh. These chickens are purchased one day after birth and fed until approximately 45 days old. At this point, they are sold to contracted customers.

The third aspect of the farm is in its early stages. This involves the growing of various vegetables along with mangos and lemons, which are grafted for an enhanced taste. Additionally, the mango trees will only grow to a height of six feet. Both will start to produce after two years. By restricting the height of mango trees the losses of fruit should be minimised.

I was quite impressed with how well organized the small farm was and with the level of expertise and commitment the local partner brought to the project.

I had dinner with the partner and his family.

We had a lovely meal which was consumed in the traditional manner. This meant communal eating around the table using only one's right hand. The meal was chicken and, as you might expect, it was very tasty!

The End.

Having begun my journey in October, I returned to the beautiful island of Bermuda on the 29th of November. I enjoyed my first trip to West Africa with the many new experiences and the ups and downs of travel. I met many wonderful people, seen many things and still smiled through some awful transport issues!

The situations I faced made me appreciate being born and raised in Bermuda. My heart goes out to the hundreds of children I saw during my travels who do not attend school. The poverty is heart-breaking but the spirit of the people is great. They do not give up but instead they continue to push on.

I wrote this book to share my experiences during my first trip to West Africa. I was amazed, entertained, exhausted and sometimes even a little worried about the situations I found myself in.

The goal is that you will decide to visit these countries and be prepared to feel the real Africa, not dressed up for tourists, no pretty face, but the real lives of the average person being lived in front of you.

I would hope that you will be able to have the exchanges with the people as I have. To share a meal in a private home as I did in Mauritania, Senegal and The Gambia is a precious occasion as you have pierced the veil and have entered the inner sanctum of their lives.

Don't be afraid to ride in the sept-place car or on the moto. These are as commonplace as public transport back home. Leave your inhibitions at home and open up to new experiences.

Lastly share...share your experiences with your family, friends and even enemies, if you have any. Our travel to Africa at the end of the day is about bridging the divide and creating greater understanding amongst us. Step out, step up and help to make a smaller better world.

I hope you have enjoyed *Travels with Terry!*

ABOUT THE AUTHOR

THE HONOURABLE TERRY Lister is a retired accountant, realtor, politician. Having served years in these capacities, in November 2014 Mr. Lister took as his vocation, travelling, on a regular basis. Since that time, he has travelled to every country in Central and South America, except for one nation. Since October 2017 he has been to 18 African nations.

Mr. Lister has continually stated that travel provides the best education possible. In this book he shares his experiences in West Africa with the view to encourage others to feel free to go, see, taste and enjoy this part of the world.